SOUTH ASIAN DANCE

THE BRITISH EXPERIENCE

Contents

Choreography and Dance, 1997, Vol 4(2), pp. 1–4
Reprints available directly from the publisher
Photocopying permitted by license only

South Asian Dance: The British Experience

Alessandra Iyer

An issue of *Choreography and Dance* specifically devoted to South Asian dance in Britain has been long overdue. The traditional 'classical' dances of the subcontinent (the use of Western categories does not always accurately describe non-Western artistic forms but it serves the purpose of giving an intelligible, shorthand explanation) have undergone fission, have been deconstructed and have become part of a contemporary dance idiom. Some of the most innovative work has taken place because of interaction of dancers from other traditions with Western (or Western trained) contemporary dancers and/or because it was conceived in a global context. The British experience has been very important in connection with such developments. Some readers may find ambiguity in the phrase 'British experience' and some, especially non-British readers, may wonder what exactly South Asian dance is.

Let us start from the beginning. Until recently South Asian dance was a term unknown to either practitioners or audiences. South Asian dance was known as 'Indian' or even as 'Asian' dance. The problem is, of course, that the India of pre-independence does not reflect modern political boundaries. The whole geographical area of the subcontinent is no longer just India. The term 'Asian' is too vague and it cannot refer only to people from or with roots in the subcontinent. South Asia refers to the whole of the subcontinent, regardless of its political subdivisions. South Asian dance is thus a shorthand term to indicate the dance traditions of the subcontinent. Some of these are 'classical' such as Bharata Natyam and Kathak; others are 'folk'. Kathak is practised in both India and Pakistan; Bharata Natyam is practised in India and in Sri Lanka, Singapore, Malaysia . . . . Hence the necessity of abandoning the term Indian.

But what do we mean by British experience? It is not the way British people perceive South Asian dance. This may be part of the 'experience', but it is not its main import. Quite simply, the British experience of South Asian dance is the work and contribution of South Asian dance practitioners based in Britain and working primarily in a British/European context. In other words, it represents the vicissitudes of South Asian dance in Britain. What happens when different cultures and their dance arts come in contact and live side by side? They inevitably change one another. How? This is what this issue of *Choreography and Dance* is about to explore.

About 15 years ago the Academy of Indian Dance, brainchild of the then British based Kathakali/Mohini Attam dancer Tara Rajkumar, held a seminar at the Commonwealth Institute, London, on the topic "*The Contribution of Indian Dance to British Culture*". The following year – same organiser, same venue – another seminar was held and this time the discussion topic was "*The Place of Indian*

Dance in British Culture" (fifteen years ago political correctness was unknown and 'South Asian' was only used in University departments that dealt with 'the languages and culture of South Asia' as opposed to the more old fashioned 'Indology'). In those days, South Asian dancers in Britain strove to be perceived and accepted as mainstream artists emphasising the purity and authenticity of their training in their own classical forms. It was for the purpose of providing back up, training and support that the Academy of Indian Dance was created in London in 1979 (it was subsequently to shift its emphasis to increasing the practice, understanding and appreciation of South Asian dance and related performing arts.)

Fifteen years later, some of the changes that have taken place have been so radical and so rapid that some people are no longer able to recognise South Asian dance forms in the way these are practised and presented. There has been a surge of dance activity aimed at expanding and merging forms, rejecting traditional content and seeking to be more attuned to contemporary life while articulating the specificity of being British and working in Britain. And yet, in the background, there is also a call to adhere to traditional values, to preserve the authenticity of the traditions and most of all, to resist facile dilutions. The resulting landscape is composite.

Situations are constantly in a state of flux and there is no feeling of self complacency when the achievements of the past decades are reviewed. There is a sense of unrest, some feeling of having had to give up some aspects of the tradition deserving to be expanded and worked upon, only because of the inability of non-Asian audiences to grasp the meaning of those aspects. But are the dancers entirely blameless on the question of accessibility? And what if the decision to concentrate on, for example, the pure dance alone, were dictated by a genuine desire to explore its potential?

Young British South Asian dancers of today insist that expansion and innovation come from within their traditional practice and are not willing to compromise their artistic integrity. Young dancers of today are also better trained then their counterparts of a decade or two ago. A number of organisations and schools have sprung up over the past 15/20 years which concentrate on the training of youngsters who wish to acquire proficiency in the classical dance traditions of the subcontinent. Some of these schools have been singlehandedly run by committed individual teachers, whose work has been very much a labour of love and who are yet to be given the recognition they deserve.

The problems faced by the young South Asian dancers of today are somewhat different from those faced in the past by their now senior colleagues. The expectations of British audiences have changed. There is a demand for quality and high standards which was not there before, thanks to the concerted effort and work done by dancers, choreographers and teachers.

One of the issues not yet addressed in Britain is the existence of different pockets of South Asian artists somewhat disconnected and not quite interacting, as well as other artists from Asian regions other than South Asia, Afro-Caribbeans and so on. They rarely come together in a genuine effort to communicate and explore each other's forms without the mediation of the white man's culture. Multiculturalism in Britain has very much to do with the white, male, European culture vis à vis other cultures which have no time for each other and are engaged in a dialogue only with the white establishment. Occasionally this turns into com-

petition for attention. A South Asian artist that has attempted a new kind of interaction is Mallika Sarabhai, a Bharata Natyam dancer who worked with Peter Badejo,
whose dance vocabulary draws from the richness and complexities of African
forms. But Sarabhai is Indian, not British based. In India, Padma Subrahmanyam
choreographed a Bharata Nrityam piece to traditional Japanese koto music. She
even composed a piece for gamelan played in Singapore in 1992. This kind of
exploration has not had any impact in Britain as yet. There is still a degree of
uncertainty and insecurity within the South Asian community and all other non-
white communities for that matter, almost a fear of losing identity if they were to
interact artistically with one another, without Western culture as a reference point.

In this issue South Asian dancers, Western contemporary dancers, writers and
academics come together to talk about the British experience, with the dancers
and choreographers specifically emphasising their own personal involvement.
Reginald Massey and Naseem Khan give us some background history of South
Asian dance in Britain. Both writers, whose approaches could not be more different, have been involved in the South Asian dance scene for some decades. They
were personally acquainted with the pioneers Uday Shankar and Ram Gopal.
Naseem trained as a Bharata Natyam dancer and was at the forefront in
campaigning for recognition of the 'minority arts'. MAAS (Minority Arts Advi-
sory Service) was her brainchild and so were a number of other important events
and organisations.

Shobana Jeyasingh talks about her concept of choreography and her attempt to
create work that explores new themes and subjects using a Bharata Natyam
technique ultimately thinking in terms of dance rather than specific forms. Shobana
has consciously decided to bracket off the expressive, mimetic portion of Bharata
Natyam, known as *abhinaya*. Her work has been acclaimed as innovative,
creative and accessible. Here she focuses on one of her best choreographic
efforts, *Making of Maps,* which won great praise when it was first shown in 1992.

Valli Subbiah, another well known Bharata Natyam dancer, questions the
exclusion of *abhinaya*, feeling that shutting a door does not make the problem
behind that door disappear. She argues for the necessity of preserving the
'maargam', the traditional sequence of repertoire, in order to continue to train
capable dancers.

Nilima Devi talks about her experience of teaching and choreographing Kathak
ever since she moved to Leicester almost two decades ago. She feels that much of
the work done by dancers and teachers has not really been noticed, the 'experts'
being engaged in fruitless discussions about what is innovative and what is traditional. Meanwhile audiences have been enjoying themselves and continue to do
so, perfectly able to understand what they are seeing.

Richard Alston is a well known English contemporary choreographer. In 1993
Alston created '*Delicious Arbour*' for the Shobana Jeyasingh Company and the work
was well received. It is usual for South Asian dancers to be asked about their collaborative work with Western dancers, less usual for a Western dancer/choreog-
rapher to have a chance to talk about South Asian dance from his or her
perspective. Alston's views may sometimes be strikingly unilateral but his overall
attitude is that of someone who sees the collaboration, and collaborative work in
general, in a positive light. Only time will tell whether this was truly more than
a well meant singular experiment. Alston's caution is admirable.

Vena Gheerawo speaks for the youngest dancers who are just beginning to perform professionally around the country. Her passion is obvious, so is the willingness to explore without compromising integrity. Young South Asian dancers have found in Vena a most sensitive and articulate representative. Vena's training in Bharata Nrityam and her research in the rich vocabulary of the dance of the *Nāṭyaśāstra* colours her approach to dance, giving her flexibility in more than one sense. Her emphasis on holism and individuality is significant.

Andrée Grau, dance anthropologist, tells us about the teaching of South Asian dance in tertiary education. Her analysis is lucid. It is important to be able to look at things objectively and see what has gone wrong and where. If there is at times a feeling of having achieved much, this is in fact not supported by the factual evidence. Is South Asian dance really being given a chance in College/University education? What is its role? Are the few existing courses tokenistic? Can the training of South Asian dancers be formalised at Higher Education level? This question is crucial if one is to say that South Asian dance is truly part of mainstream British culture.

Christopher Bannerman, contemporary choreographer, dancer and academic is very enthusiastic about multicultural interaction. When he tells us that his encounter with South Asian dance was a profound experience, one can sense the empathy and depth of feeling with which this statement is made. Christopher Bannerman is, however, extremely rational in his approach and has a vision for the future, not specifically linked to South Asian dance, although certainly encompasses and gives it room to grow. In this respect his contribution to dance is of inestimable value.

For obvious reasons the work of many people could not be examined here nor could all the opinions of those actively involved with South Asian dance be recorded. It was not possible, for instance, either to interview or seek a contribution from Nahid Siddiqui whose work using the Kathak form has broken new ground in terms of choreographic concepts, whose skills as a dancer and choreographer are equally matched by her skills as exacting teacher. Young Sonia Kundi, who creates waves whenever she performs her immaculate Kathak, is entirely a product of Nahid's careful training. One must also mention the work of Priya Pawar and her group of committed Odissi students, the work of Prakash Yadagudde who has taught a number of youngsters at the Bharatiya Vidya Bhavan, among whom Vena Gheerawo, who has contributed to this issue.

The British experience of South Asian dance is, on the whole, extremely positive. British South Asian dancers can stand on their own feet and are at the forefront of new developments. Their creativity, their competence, their talent, passion and commitment have sustained their efforts, often with insufficient backing from officialdom and funding bodies. It is high time that this excellent work be taken notice of, discussed and shared with the international community of dancers and dance workers, teachers and researchers.

Choreography and Dance, 1997, Vol 4(2), pp. 5–17
Reprints available directly from the publisher
Photocopying permitted by license only

South Asian Dance: The Traditional/Classical Idioms

Alessandra Iyer

Brief History

In order to be able to contextualise in dance terms the British experience of South Asian dance, it is necessary to give a short introduction to the traditional/classical dance idioms that go under the collective name 'South Asian dance'.

It is an oft repeated formula that the dances of the subcontinent, in particular those that in the West we would categorise as classical, are rooted in a tradition that is undoubtedly very ancient, going back two thousand years. This has, on occasion, superficially been taken to mean that the traditional dances of the subcontinent are two thousand years old. This could not be further from the truth and it has the unfortunate result of turning South Asian dances into museum pieces in the eyes of Westerners. We have evidence of a continuous practice of dance for thousands of years, yet what is danced now is not at all what was danced two thousand years ago.

Let us first of all clarify the question of 'classical' versus 'folk'. This categorisation is not indigenous to the subcontinent. It was introduced in the 20th century when the dances of India were revived, out of a need to give them equal status to that of the Western classical dance tradition (ballet). For centuries, in the subcontinent, there had been a tradition of formalised and sophisticated dance forms whose practice had been codified in works (not necessarily written down) which went by the name of *śāstra*. Thus dances would be classified as sastraic and non-sastraic. The first known treatise was the *Nāṭyaśāstra*, on the date of which there is no consensus, though scholars agree that it cannot be later than the 4th century A.D.[1] The *Nāṭyaśāstra* took stock of what was the contemporary practice and gave precise guidelines about how to put on a dramatic performance. In this work dance was seen as integral part of drama, together with music and poetry. The *Nāṭyaśāstra* has a whole chapter on the technique of *karaṇa* (dance movement units) out of which dances were choreographed The number of dance *karaṇa* is given as 108, but there are many more *karaṇa* formed by putting together smaller movement units involving only the legs (*cārī*). The *Nāṭyaśāstra* calls dance either *nṛtta* or *tāṇḍava*. This technique of dance became obsolete a long time ago. We have evidence, especially through sculpture, that it was pan-Asian, because of its link with religion, in particular to the god Śiva. The *karaṇa* were his gift to the

---

[1] Cfr. M. Bose 1970, *Classical Indian dancing: a glossary,* Calcutta: General Printers and Publishers, pp. 1–4.

world.[2] The movement material of the *Nāṭyaśāstra* is so varied and rich that one wonders, on the basis of historical evidence of lively contacts and exchanges between India and neighbouring and faraway countries, whether some of the movements codified in this text originated outside India, entered the subcontinent and were later on recycled within and outside India. Fascinating and intriguing though this question may be, this is not at all the right context for exploring its implications.

Many more treatises and works were composed after the *Nāṭyaśāstra*, using the *Nāṭyaśāstra* itself as a model. The tradition of the *Nāṭyaśāstra* came to be known as *mārgī*, literally 'of the high way'. But there were also regional, local traditions, known as *deśi*. These were not the equivalent of folk dance. They were highly sophisticated forms, with their own *śāstra*. The *Nāṭyaśāstra* implies, without calling them so, that *deśi* forms coexist with the form it describes – which later texts referred to as *mārgī*. This points to the great variety of forms that has always existed in the subcontinent, from very early times.

After the *Nāṭyaśāstra*, other treatises paid greater attention to the *deśi* forms and reference to the *Nāṭyaśāstra* was only by lipservice. Slowly, the different strands of sastraic dance were uniformly codified into *nṛtta* (pure dance) and *nṛtya* (expressive dance) which incorporated the *abhinaya*, that is, the mimetic portions originally pertaining only to *nāṭya* (drama). The original *nāṭya* was Sanskrit drama, but later the term came to refer to dance-dramas which made use of the Indian vernaculars for their songs and spoken dialogue. All present day 'classical' forms have retained this internal subdivision into *nṛtta* and *nṛtya*. It is not possible to go through the whole history of the development of the 'classical' styles of South Asian dance. Suffice it to say that they are firmly rooted in a rich tradition of sastraic dance in both its temple and court variety. They represent the living *deśi* tradition. The so called 'folk' forms, also regional in character and constantly interacting with the more polished regional 'classical' traditions are also an important part of the South Asian dance heritage and much effort has been put into preserving and even reviving some of these forms. The *karaṇa* of the *Nāṭyaśāstra*, which have had such a great influence on the development of the visual and performing arts of the whole of Hindu/Buddhist Asia can still be seen sporadically in all the South Asian dance forms, including some 'folk' dance movements. They have recently been revived after a painstaking research carried out by Dr Padma Subrahmanyam, who has reconstructed them and re-introduced them into dance practice.

I mentioned earlier temple and court dance as well as dance-dramas. The South Asian dance traditions are, by and large, connected with religion. This statement needs qualifying. The religious connection was very strong in the *mārgī* as well as in the *deśi* traditions. Some dancing was practised in temples as part of religious worship by a special group of women known as *devadāsī*. Some other dance forms were practised by large groups of male dancers during festival times in the form of dance-dramas with a ritual purpose. The *Nāṭyaśāstra* does not mention temple dancing; it probably became institutionalised in later times possibly coinciding with the growth of devotional movements, known as *bhakti*. The spread of *bhakti* fostered temple building activities, with temples becoming centres of

---

[2]   This is narrated in chapter 4 of the *Nāṭyaśāstra*, where śiva after seeing the charming dramatic performance put on by Brahma suggests dance should be added (NS 4, vv. 11–16).

patronage for the arts. There was, however, also a tradition of dance associated with the courts. This was centred on entertainment, but it was not entirely devoid of religious significance. There was never a great divide between the two traditions in ancient India. Also, the patron of both temple and court was the ruler who was seen, in Hindu India, as the representative on earth of the divinity.

Of course, when Islam made an impact on the subcontinent, reaching its zenith under the Mughals[3] it did not countenance temple worship nor did it accord Muslim rulers the mantle of divinity. The dance tradition of Muslim South Asia was predominantly that of the ruler's court. However, there was a distinctive Hindu substratum. Hinduism and Islam coexisted influencing the way the arts developed.[4] Today, South Asian dance has come down to us in distinct regional styles, which have the status of classical dance. By the beginning of the 20th century, for historical reasons (see the articles in this issue by Reginald Massey and Nazeem Khan) the highly sophisticated dances of the subcontinent were in danger of extinction. However, the indefatigable efforts of a few pioneers and committed individuals ensured their survival, revival and finally transition to the modern stage. These styles are now the traditional idioms of South Asian dances. Their history tells us that South Asian dance has been constantly evolving, merging into new forms. The history of South Asian dance has never and could never be static. These traditional/classical styles of today are the basis for the new styles and forms of tomorrow. To an extent, these styles are today's *mārgī* form. Perhaps it would not be inappropriate to say that British South Asian dance is one of the new *deśi* forms.

The Classical Styles

The classical styles are today known as follows:

1. Bharata Natyam
2. Kathakali
3. Odissi
4. Kathak
5. Mohini Attam
6. Manipuri
7. Chhau
8. Kuchipudi

There are also other forms; a very short description of the styles follows.

---

[3]   Islam first came to India with the Arab traders in the 8th c. A.D. Three centuries later Muslim rule began in the North, with the coming of the Turks, Afghans and Persians. The first Delhi sultanate was established in the 12th century.

[4]   It is very apparent that many elements of Hindu origin continued in Islamic art, even, for example, in the tradition of miniature painting which seems to be ultimately based on Hindu principles of composition (cfr. A. Boner and B. Baumer and Pandit Rath Sharma 1982 *Vastusūtra Upaniṣad* Delhi: Motilal Banarsidass, p. 29).

Bharata Natyam

This is a form associated with South India, in particular the Tamil speaking region. It has inherited the traditional repertoire of the *devadāsī-s* (temple dancers). It is essentially a solo form. Its main position is a very low demiplie (*ardhamaṇḍalī* or *araimandi*) with a good turn out of the knees. The form is very geometric, with an emphasis on triangles. Its dance units are known as *aḍavu-s*. The drum accompaniment is provided by the *mridangam*, the music traditionally associated with this form is South Indian classical (Carnatic) music. The dance conductor is known as *naṭṭuvaṉ* and he (she) keeps the time with cymbals and spoken syllables (*sorkaṭṭu*).

Figure 1   Bharatiya Vidya Bhavan student Esha Dasgupta, Bharata Natyam. Photo: Ray Clark.

Kathakali

An all male dance drama form, Kathakali comes from the South West of India, the region known as Kerala. It has a strong martial art basis (Kathakali dancers are often practitioners of *Kalari Payattu,* a traditional martial art from Kerala). Its main position is a wide stance with the weight on the side of the soles of the feet, known as *parśvakuñcita pāda*. Kathakali dancers/actors have a highly developed language of mime, with hand gestures that allow them to indicate the endings of verbal forms and nouns. Their make up is an art form in itself, with a range of colours for the different characters. The make up gives the illusion of wearing a mask and may have developed from masks. The musical accompaniment is a type of Carnatic singing known as *sopana* style, very slow and majestic. The drums used are the *chenda* and *maddala,* of a cylindrical shape and with two drum faces. The former is played with one hand and one stick, the latter with both hands on the respective side.

Figure 2   Tara Raj kumar (right) and Chandrasekhar (left), Kathakali. Photo: Ray Clark.

Odissi

This form is from the East of India and it was at one time danced by the *mahārī-s* (temple dancers) and the *gotipua*-s (young boys that danced dressed as women at religious festivals). Its basic stances are the *chowka* or square with legs wide apart and knees fully turned out and the *tribhaṅga*, a position in which the body shows three bends (neck, waist, hip). Thus it shows a combination of strength and extreme grace. The torso is very flexible with a variety of subtle, side movements. The music of Odissi is known as Odissi music, although nowadays North Indian classical music is used. The long poem *Gītāgovinda* by Jayadeva is by far the most popular repertoire piece.

Figure 3   Priya Pawar, Odissi. Photo: Ray Clark.

Figure 4 Odissi Group Students Showcase, Academy of Indian Dance. Courtesy of the Academy of Indian Dance. Photo: Sheila Geraghty.

Kathak

The word means story teller and originally *kathakar-s* were bands of story tellers that went from village to village to tell tales of the gods in an accessible form. It is a dance form that has been wholly shaped by court patronage. There are different *gharana-s* or schools within Kathak, most notably the Lucknow and the Jaipur *gharana*. Its main position is a straight stance (*samasthāna*) and its characteristics are the fast footwork and the pirouettes or *chakkar-s*. Its musical accompaniment is provided by *tabla* (two cylinder drum) and North Indian vocal music. Kathak dancers wear hundreds of small bells round the ankles, to emphasise their footwork. These are known as *ghungroo-s*.

Figure 5   Alpana Sengupta, Kathak. Photo: Ray Clark.

Figure 6   Nilima Devi, Kathak. Courtesy of Nilima Devi.

Figure 7   Nilima Devi, Kathak. Courtesy of Nilima Devi.

Mohini Attam

The name literally means 'Dance of the enchantress Mohini'. It is a solo female dance form from Kerala and shows influence from both Kathakali and Bharata Natyam. It is characterised by a roundness of movement and swaying of the arms and torso reminiscent of palm trees in the wind. The music is classical Carnatic; the language of its songs is Malayalam. Mohini Attam dancers wear their hair in a knot on the side of the head, which adds charm.

Figure 8   Bharati Shivaji, Mohini Attam. Photo: Ray Clark.

Manipuri

This style comes from the region of Manipur, in Eastern India and shows some affinity with Burmese dance. The movements are very fluid and the ground is never struck with force. The male form is characterised by leaps, spins and forceful jumps. The body is moved in a very undulating way. There is no counterpart of the *ardhamaṇḍalī* of Bharata Natyam or Mohini Attam.

Figure 9   Manipuri Group. Photo: Ray Clark.

Chhau

Until 15 years ago Chhau was regarded as a folk form and was not well known outside its native Orissa, Purulia and Bengal. There are 3 forms (Seraikella and Purulia with mask, Mayurbhanj without masks). Its basis is very martial (being linked to the martial art traditions of the region). The style of narrative uses the body in full rather than relying on hand gesture and facial expression, as do Southern styles such as Kathakali. There is an emphasis on leg movements, with springs and jumps that can be quite spectacular.

Kuchipudi

From Andhra Pradesh, Kuchipudi started off as an all male dance-drama performed on specific occasions. Later, women began to dance it and it was further modified for the modern stage when dancers began to treat it as a solo dance presenting only excerpts from dance-dramas. Its basic technique is akin to Bharata Natyam but the footwork is faster and there is less emphasis on geometric lines. Dancers may do their own singing and characteristic items involve dancing on a tray or dancing while balancing a small pot on the head. Its music is classical Carnatic.

The above are only notes just to remind readers of the main classical styles that go under the name of South Asian dance. But there are many others. Example are the dance drama traditions such as Yakshagana of Karnataka, Bhagavata Mela of Tamilnadu which are 'classical' in terms of their sophistication, though their function is still that of ritual performance. They are rarely seen outside their villages; this is the case with Bhagavata Mela still performed in Melattur by Brahmin boys as part of the celebrations for the festival of Lord Narasimha.

Dance-drama (formerly known as ballet) is also a new category which denotes all group performances that have been put together since the classical dances of the subcontinent were revived. There are also the contemporary dance styles evolved by Uday Shankar and Tagore and more recently by Manjusree Sirkar. Finally there are a host of community/folk dances whose purpose is essentially celebratory (Raas Garba, Bhangra etc.). Thus, contemporary South Asian dancers have a very wide range of movement styles and traditions to draw upon in order to forge their own idioms.

Choreography and Dance, 1997, Vol 4(2), pp. 19–23
Reprints available directly from the publisher
Photocopying permitted by license only

In Praise of the Pioneers

Reginald Massey

Indian dance, music and art are now widely accepted in Britain. Local education authorities and arts bodies allocate funding, several teachers earn a living teaching it and many cultural organisations hold regular classes and workshops in London and other cities. Moreover, the interest is not confined to Asians alone; people of all ages from non-Asian backgrounds are learning Indian dance with great interest and enthusiasm.

But this has not happened overnight and must never be taken for granted by those who now practise Indian dance in Britain either professionally or as a part-time activity. It has been a difficult, uphill struggle covering a period of several decades; many have dedicated their lives to the cause of propagating Indian dance in this country. It is in their honour that I set down this record of achievement.

First things first. The British ruled India and, as has always happened, the norms of the rulers were imposed upon those who were ruled. A parallel can be drawn with the Roman conquest of Britain. Because of the conquest, Britain became, in effect, a 'civilised' country. By the time the Romans left, the British tribes had exchanged their fur and woad for cloth. Indeed, some might well have been clad in cottons from India, for the Roman Empire was an important market for Indian textiles.

In Victorian times the British took the business of the 'White man's burden' very seriously. Pax Romana was replaced by Pax Britannica in their mission to civilise the world, including, of course, India. Roads and railways were constructed; English law was enforced. *Thuggee* and *sati* were stamped out. The English language became paramount. European medicine replaced the Ayurvedic and Unani systems. In education, Shakespeare and Shelley displaced Kalidasa and Jayadeva. All that was British was unquestionably the best and, by implication, all that was Indian inferior.

It is therefore not surprising that when the British saw erotic sculptures adorning temples and *devadāsī-s* (temple dancers) plying their trade within the temple precincts, they condemned Hinduism and all its works. It is a fact that in 1927 in Madras Presidency alone, which was part of British India, there were 200,000 temple prostitutes. Mahatma Gandhi lamented that many temples were "no better than brothels".

Apart from men like Sir William Jones who founded the Asiatic Society of Bengal in 1784, few British administrators had time for Indian art. The exotic Hindu temple dance of South India was something the average European could not comprehend. Hence it was ignored. The active opposition came from upper-caste 'enlightened' Hindus who were clearly embarrassed by what was happening in the temples. They could not see it was the *devadāsī* who had kept alive a great art.

Dāsī Aṭṭam, the classical dance of the *devadāsī-s* which had been handed down from mother to daughter for many generations, was not something that decent, educated Indians discussed in the presence of their children. High caste Hindus certainly did not allow their daughters to have any contact with a dance art practised by prostitutes. But the poets, as often happens, thought differently.

In 1901 the Bengali poet Tagore founded Santiniketan with assistance from the English educator Leonard Elmhirst who had founded Dartington Hall in Devon. Tagore emphasised the importance of music, dance, drama, painting and sculpture in the process of education and persuaded leading musicians, dancers and artists to teach at Santiniketan. Later, in 1930 the Kerala poet Vallathol established the Kerala Kalamandalam to fulfil his dream of reinstating the Kathakali dance drama to its former glory. Such was Vallathol's persistence that, when he could not raise funds from the usual sources, he set up a lottery, cajoled his many friends and admirers to buy tickets and with the profits started his dance school.

In the province of Madras the stigma of temple prostitution continued for a long time and it was only when two Brahmins, E. Krishna Iyer and Rukmini Devi started their dance crusade that *Dāsī Aṭṭam* became 'respectable'. In the process *Dāsī Aṭṭam* was rechristened 'Bharata Natyam'. I use the word "rechristened" advisedly. For, rather like the early Christians adopting pagan festivals and making them 'respectable', in the early decades of this century the Brahmin establishment of South India Brahminized the *Dāsī Aṭṭam* into Bharata Natyam. "What's in a name?" a Shakespeare character queried going on to suggest that it made no difference. But it does.

Since Indian dance had to struggle for recognition and identity in India itself, one can well imagine its position in Britain during the period before the Second World War. The dance scene, as a whole, was not as vibrant and varied as it is now (even though Ninette de Valois had founded the Royal Ballet School in 1931 and the Royal Academy of Dancing had been operating since 1920). It is worth recalling that classical ballet grew and was nurtured in Italy, France and Russia and it was only the dedication of Ninette de Valois, Marie Rambert, Frederick Ashton, Alicia Markova, Margot Fonteyn and other stalwarts that eventually put British ballet on the dance map of the world. British dancers, choreographers and dance enthusiasts were too engrossed in their own problems to be concerned about foreign forms and traditions.

However, a few Western dancers were captivated by Indian dance. During the early years of this century the American Ruth St Denis toured the world with her 'Oriental' *Radha Dance* and when she and her husband Ted Shawn started their famous dance centre at Jacob's Pillow they welcomed Indian dancers there. Martha Graham had the highest regard for Indian dance. Inspired by the Krishna legend, Fokine and Cocteau created *Le Dieu Bleu* in which the god was danced by Nijinsky with Karsavina as Radha.

In the twenties the great Pavlova toured India and the Far East. In Madras, her Indian hosts informed her that Indian dance had all but died out and what was left was not worth watching. Ever a searcher, she persevered and visited temples where the *devadāsī-s* still danced. It was Pavlova who advised Rukmini Devi to give up studying Russian ballet and to rediscover the dance heritage of her own country. Thus Rukmini Devi became the first and most significant dancer of South India who was not a *devadāsī*. She founded the Kalakshetra Academy which has produced many of India's foremost dancers; in her personal life she broke with tradition and married an Englishman. Pavlova also inspired Menaka to become the first Kathak dancer who was not a *bai* or *tavaif* (courtesan). Before Menaka no decent Hindu, Muslim or Sikh family would have anything to do with Kathak, which, it was widely believed, belonged to the *kothā-s* or whorehouses.

The most celebrated personality that Pavlova inspired, indeed discovered, was Uday Shankar who was the first Indian dancer to make an impact in the West. The Shankar family were art conscious and even though Shankar senior was a lawyer and former minister in the state of Jhalawar, he often produced and directed plays. The family was a product of what has come to be called the Indian Renaissance. It started in Bengal, ironically, under the influence of the new liberal British education system which introduced upper caste Bengalis to the heady ideas propagated by freethinking poets such as Byron and Shelley. The first Indian 'intellectuals' in the European sense of the word, were upper caste Bengali Hindus.

As a progressive Bengali Brahmin, Shankar senior encouraged his son Uday to fulfil his ambition which was to become a painter; and so Uday was sent to study at the Royal College of Art in London under Sir William Rothenstein. But the gods had other plans.

In 1924, Shankar senior was in London and organised a stage show for charity. He asked his son to help out with some dancing, which Uday did quite willingly. Pavlova came to the show and was so impressed by the young student's talent that she asked him to join her in two short ballets on Indian themes that she was keen to produce. *The Hindu Wedding* and *Radha and Krishna* were significant landmarks not only because they gave Uday Shankar his first experience as a professional dancer (he danced Krishna to Pavlova's Radha) but also because he gained an understanding of the technical aspects of ballet production from a guru of Pavlova's stature.

Shankar was with Pavlova for a year and a half and then launched out on his own in Paris. In 1929 he returned to India, studied Bharata Natyam and Kathakali in the South, sketched the temple dance sculptures and friezes and filmed many folk dances. He collected an accomplished group of dancers and musicians, which he called the Uday Shankar Company of Hindu Dancers and Musicians, and embarked for Europe. The whole Shankar family was involved in this self-financed and privately sponsored cultural enterprise. Uday Shankar's mother and his three younger brothers Rajendra, Debendra and Ravi were part of the company. The very thought of such an undertaking leaves one breathless.

Uday Shankar was driven by destiny; whenever the company appeared it was crowned with stupendous success. For many years Shankar was based in England in the picturesque setting of Dartington Hall and it was from here that he and his company made forays far and wide. It was chiefly because of Uday Shankar that India's dance and music gained worldwide respect. This was particularly true in Britain.

Ravi Shankar, the youngest of the Shankar brothers, who first appeared on stage as a dancer in his brother's productions has written: "It is a rare thing for a person with no formal training to become a great dancer and a pioneer in the art as well . . . He appeared, really like a god, filled with an intense power and overwhelming beauty. To me he was a superman." I recall writing in the London *Times*: "In the history of dance he will be remembered for the professional standards he set for Indian ballet, and for evolving a new style . . . Shankar nurtured a galaxy of talent which, in later years, profoundly influenced the performing arts of the country . . . More recently, however, he was criticised by the orthodox purists for having the audacity to innovate and fashion was in their favour. He died largely disillusioned but a lord of the dance nonetheless".[1]

The other genius to bring Indian dance to Britain and the West was Ram Gopal. He had been trained and honed by gurus such as Kathakali's Kunju Kurup and Bharata Natyam's Meenakshi Sundaram Pillai. He was a major dancer in India. Gopal first toured abroad with the American dancer La Meri and later, on his own, he took America by storm. In 1939 his London debut at the Aldwych Theatre heralded a meteoric career in this country. He was invited to meet Queen Mary; leading figures of the world of ballet became his friends; and in 1948 Nijinksy himself came to see him dance at the Saville Theatre.

Ram Gopal had charisma and the ability to influence people and to turn their hearts and minds towards things Indian. Markova danced Radha to his Krishna and there was a time when his name was synonymous with that of Indian classical dance. Ram Gopal was also very cosmopolitan: he lived well and he lived in style. In the sixties I worked with him for a short while and had the opportunity of studying him at close quarters. His luxurious flat in Chelsea was adorned with the most tasteful art from both East and West and he was visited by leading writers, poets, painters, film directors, actors and musicians.

I believe that Ram Gopal is proof that dancers transcend race, style and technique. To use his words, theirs is a "universal language of the body in any rhythm of the dance, be it Eastern or Western".[2] Of course, his background has much to do with his catholic views. His father was a cultivated Rajput from North India, his mother a Burmese lady of great beauty, and he was brought up in South India. As a boy he first danced in a palace in Mysore. His cultural roots are thus rich and varied.

Over the years, Ram Gopal has worked ceaselessly for the cause of Indian dance, not only in Britain where he made his home, but also in India. A living legend of the dance, Ram Gopal now winters in his beloved Venice by the Grand Canal. Diaghilev lies on an island near Venice and I remember being taken by Ram Gopal to visit the island. He laid flowers on Diaghilev's grave with tears in his eyes. For his services to the art of dance Ram Gopal deserves to be honoured, by both India and Britain. Unfortunately, this has not yet happened.

The work of critics such as Arnold Haskell and Fernau Hall, the work of artists such as Eilean Pearcey and editors such as Mary Clarke of *The Dancing Times* created an atmosphere of acceptance and understanding in Britain. I would be failing in my duty if I did not record their contribution towards the present status of Indian dance in Britain. Also, *The Arts that Britain Ignores*, an incisive report by Naseem Khan, made educational and funding bodies aware of their responsibility towards a number of 'ethnic' art forms including Indian dance. The early dance promoters (Ayana Deva Angadi, Birendra Shankar and Ramesh Patel among others) played their part and must not be forgotten. The future augurs well.

---

[1]   September 29, 1977.

[2]   *Rhythm in the Heavens.*

Figure 10   Ram Gopal. Courtesy of ADiTi. Photo: Channel 4.

Choreography and Dance, 1997, Vol 4(2), pp. 25–30
Reprints available directly from the publisher
Photocopying permitted by license only

South Asian Dance in Britain 1960–1995

Naseem Khan

The history of what, until the last decade, was called Indian dance has been a troubled, dramatic and difficult story. If it were a film, it would be a saga. If it were a piece of music, it would be a panoramic symphony with plentiful stretches of percussion and the darker range of strings. This brief survey attempts to dissect the elements that have influenced its passage. Inevitably it has had to simplify, and omit some of the players. It is hoped that anyone who notices this will be generous and appreciate the difficulty of the task.

First making an impact in Britain in the 1920s with Uday Shankar, Indian dance played the part of the colourful stranger for its first three decades of life. Troupes came from India in a gradually increasing stream, some staying several months and teaching a handful of fascinated English dancers a few selected items. Some were extremely illustrious, such as the highly creative Mrinalini Sarabhai.

Ram Gopal made his first appearance in the London stage in 1939, to rapturous notices, full house for a three week run and an invitation to take tea with the Queen Mother. But the dancers were birds of passage and press reviews reflected a bemused if not unfriendly view of their work. Exotic, oriental, vaguely spiritual, it was felt to come from a foreign world with foreign values and aesthetics that were a closed book.

Dancers themselves had not colluded in this view. A number, like Shanta Rao, Krishnan Kutty and Ram Gopal himself had seriously tried to put down roots and make a place for themselves in Western culture. But time was not on their side. There was no Arts Council until the late 1940s to help cushion the risk and, even if there had been, it is doubtful that it would have regarded Indian dance as a fit object for British patronage. Survivors of those early years remember them as years of struggle and huge financial uncertainty.

However, the 1960s began to see the beginnings of change and a cautious measure of growth. Two factors were the main ones at work. Firstly, there was an overall change in the response to Indian culture in general. The great sitarist, Pandit Ravi Shankar, had played at the Edinburgh Festival in 1958, followed by his peer on the sarod, Ali Akbar Khan. Rather than being an isolated rarity as Uday Shankar had been earlier, these major performers became grounded in a wider on-going network that was just in the process of being founded.

Organisations like the Asian Music Circle (formed by Ayana Deva Angadi) were locally based with the raison d'être of introducing and interpreting Indian culture to a non-Indian society. Birendra Shankar's annual festival *Sanskritik* on the South Bank had a liberal base and planned to make friends through education and knowledge.

Lastly there were the beginnings of concerted efforts to set up viable training schools in Britain itself. In 1963 Ram Gopal had already tried to establish such a unit, opening the last of his attempts in Chelsea. Here he attempted to replicate the classical syllabus of the mother country with first rate teachers like Rina Singha (Kathak) and Zohra Sehgal (Uday Shankar style). Gopal himself, of course, taught Bharata Natyam. The classes failed ultimately because Gopal had no organisation or administrative base backing his efforts.

Three years later, a new story began. 1966 saw the first organised and long-lasting series of Indian dance classes in Britain. They were run by the Asian Music Circle which imaginatively decided to bring over a couple (husband and wife) of dancer/teachers from South India. US Krishna Rao and his wife UK Chandrabhaga Devi had been trained in Bharata Natyam in the old guru – kula tradition by one of the great gurus of the South, Meenakshi Sundaram Pillai (Ram Gopal's own guru). Their regular classes brought a new energy and focus to a sporadic, ad hoc and occasionally very frustrating scene. Pupils inspired by the Raos' unfailing enthusiasm and teaching talent made their way through the classical Bharata Natyam repertoire, eventually becoming members of a company, under the Raos, that toured dance-dramas nationally as well as to Ireland and Belgium. And while the Raos were in Britain, another event took place on the world stage that was to have enormous repercussions on the world of Indian arts in Britain.

The expulsion of Indian communities from the East African countries of Uganda, Kenya and Tanzania was deemed a huge problem by a western populace, alerted by Enoch Powell to dangers of 'swamping'. In fact, the arrival of these exiles brought not social stress but great benefit. It is commonly understood that the corner shop was saved from extinction by East African Asians. What is less often acknowledged is their effect on the arts. Having a ready made cultural construct, they needed only to set it down on British soil and set it going. In no time, there were fully fledged music schools, folk dance groups and amateur theatre companies. Even more important, there was a community with the habit of cultural consumption, in other words, an audience. Problems in developing viable arts earlier had sprung from the difficulties of attracting immigrants who came from depressed or rural areas of the subcontinent. Economic migrants aiming to establish themselves and eventually send for their families, did not have culture high on their agenda. The arrival of East African Asians changed all that overnight.

Here – almost overnight – was the support for the Bharatiya Vidya Bhavan (Institute of Indian Culture), leapfrogging, between 1972 and 1977 from a small office to a vast West London cultural centre. Here were participants for the busy organisation Nava Kala (claiming now to be Britain's oldest Indian cultural association) with its dance classes, dance displays and music performances. Here were the cast members of the energetic Gujerati theatre scene; here was a group interested in and literary activities. Here were the people that danced, in their hundreds, for the annual nine-night festival of Navaratri.

Simultaneously, a change in perception was taking place in British white society. The 1970s witnessed a series of public debates on the place and nature of the arts. Young practitioners (coming out of the 'bulge years' and a greatly increased student population) challenged old and set assumptions that sited the arts in conventional 'art houses': theatres, galleries and dance studios. New performance work made its way defiantly onto the street, into non-art venues: pubs, schools, garages, warehouses. Community arts adherents based themselves on council estates and in working class communities, seeking to engage the inhabitants to release the creativity that they passionately believed was part of every single living human being. The story of the immigrant, of the culture that was a treasured part of personal identity, was for the first time seen not as exotic but as a valid device for personal expression and survival.

In time, the funding bodies came to respond to these new facts and ideas. 'Ethnic arts' became one of the beneficiaries of the challenges to the status quo, though it took time for the Arts Council to understand that non-western arts often worked from a different dynamic; they did not always fit neatly into established funding structures.

The involvement of the Arts Council, one of the backers of the first report into ethnic arts, *The Arts Britain Ignores* (1976), meant that Indian dance was helped in its struggle to move from the world of multiculturalism (variety shows set up by Race Equality and Community Relations bodies) to the world of professional arts.

The dance that dominated aimed for authenticity, purity and classicism. In that it echoed the central thrust of dance in India itself where independence in 1947 had meant a determined restatement of the longevity of India's cultural roots. Dancers there went back to primary sources – old manuscripts and treatises and even old temples for sculptural evidence of dance poses – to assure themselves that their work was directly in line with the work of their progenitors in India's glorious past. Hence, a kind of radical conservatism was the keynote.

The teachers and dancers of the 1970s and early 1980s in Britain heeded the same tune. But greater ease with the West and awareness of the challenges it presented slowly came to result in different attitudes. Tara Rajkumar, the founder of the Academy of Indian Dance (1979), came from an unassailable classical tradition as a Mohini Attam dancer in India. Yet she rapidly came to see that Indian classical dance in Britain had to enter into a dialogue with local structures and voices. Her Academy aimed to see a fully validated syllabus for a dance degree course in Britain. Other dancers increasingly explored work in British schools, trying to find ways to fit their own practices and expectations into a setting that had rather different assumptions of what dance is and does.

It is interesting to look at the work of Pratap and Priya Pawar as one telling example of change. Pratap Pawar, who had trained at the Kathak Kendra in Delhi, had been sent to the West with his Odissi dancer wife, Priya, as cultural ambassador. In Guyana first of all , they had begun to articulate links with local practice. And although their teaching both in the West Indies and later in Britain held to its traditional line and direction, the performance work they produced began to explore overlaps, echoes and sharings. For example, they set Kathak beside Flamenco and Caribbean dance, demonstrating that rhythmical and percussive patterns were important to all of them.

The Academy of Indian Dance took a bold step in 1983 when it commissioned a dance drama that eschewed a religious or classically based theme. Choreographed by the well regarded couple from India, the Dhananjayans, it dealt with Kipling's story of Mowgli. The event featured dancers whose work was to take them into different directions later: Shobana Jeyasingh as Bagheera the panther; Pushkala Gopal as Baloo the bear; Unnikrishnan as Mowgli; and Pratap Pawar as a particularly splendid tiger Sher Khan. It created a form that could contain and sustain different classical styles (Odissi, Bharata Natyam and Kathak). As important, it addressed the knotty problem of the dance-drama form itself with its need for dramatic shaping, for a successful narrative voice via *mudra-s* (hand gestures), and for the existence of an overall rasa or mood.

The Adventures of Mowgly broke new ground by attracting uninitiated new audiences, reassured by an apparently familiar story. But it also raised concerns that are still hotly debated today. What is the place of a classical canon in a new culture? Do folk forms have a part to play in the formation of a new British based style and is there such a thing? How can Western stagecraft constructively affect Indian classical dance? The arrival of *Mowgli* on tour on mainstream stages also made the contrast between the lot of Indian dancers and Western dancers cruelly apparent. The *Mowgli* dancers were struggling to hold their own as professional dancers, and drew their strength from their Indian training rather than from immediate support. There was little infrastructure, little training, resources or support. There was a severe absence of a common language between the Indian dancers (or South Asian dancers, as they were in the process of becoming), the Western dancers and the cultural mainstream.

But the numbers of South Asian dancers anxious to devote their working life to their art were growing. How many, nobody precisely knew. Working in isolation, they were growing in curiosity and confidence in terms of their own art. Starting from classical bases, dancers such as Alpana Sengupta, Piali Ray, Chitralekha Bolar and Indira Thyagarajah were beginning to create extended pieces that examined pertinent issues: work, resettlement, the place of women. They experimented with the format, but not with the form.

Shobana Jeyasingh's experiments with Bharata Natyam began in the mid-80's in a cautious and characteristically careful way, first placing it in unison with the work of Jayachandran, an Indian dancer trained in Western contemporary dance. Steadily expanding her range and scope, she delved to increasing depths, using the agency of commissioned music by contemporary Western composers like Michael Nyman to help deconstruct the elaborate and ordered vocabulary of Bharata Natyam.

The burgeoning of the field in general was undoubtedly assisted by the establishment and work of ADiTi, the national organisation for South Asian dance. A pioneering and unusual body, it was set up after lengthy discussions amongst dancers (with Arts Council support). Run by dancers, its aim was to support them, to help the form acquire a higher profile, and generally work towards its integration, but not its absorption, into the mainstream.

Its official launch in 1991 could be seen as a symbol for the aspirations of South Asian dancers in Britain. It took place on an overcast summer's day in Bradford, ADiTi's base. Drivers and passers-by in the city centre must have been surprised to see gathering numbers of dancers in costume across the street from the major Bradford Alhambra Theatre. At a given signal, the dancers flocked across the street, to the pounding insistent thump of the Punjabi dhol. At the theatre, wave upon wave ran in unison to the large glass doors and symbolically beat on them. After the last wave, the Lord Mayor and his wife, grinning from ear to ear, flung open the doors, tossed flower petals under the advancing dancers' feet and welcomed them in. There, in the theatre's broad foyer, the varied dancers, from all styles represented in the country, performed together. Each had choreographed a small section of the same piece of music in their own style. The panorama of Bharata Natyam next to Kathak, Bhangra next to Odissi, Kathakali next to Raas Garba was

Figure 11 Shobana Jeyasingh Dance Company. *Raid* (1995). Left to right: Natasha Bakht, Jeyaverni Jeganathan, Jasmine Simhalan, Savitha Shekhar, Sowmya Gopalan. Photo: Hugo Glendinning.

a picture of unity in diversity and a vivid demonstration of the multifarious nature of what still went under the misleading single title 'South Asian dance'.

By the end of the 80s, it was clear that dancers had staked out an expanded territory. They had begun to establish courses that would equip them to work constructively in school. They had followed in the footsteps of Alpana Sengupta and become animateurs and dancers in the community. They were playing with the form, seeing what innovation might mean in practice. Dancers like Pushkala Gopal and Unnikrishnan worked with Western theatre directors (most notably Hilary Westlake) on long works like *Beauty and the Beast* that challenged their own attitudes as traditional classical dancers.

An expansionist and exciting time, it inevitably gave rise to a proportion of work that had still to find the new equation for which it was searching. 'Innovation' proved as difficult in dance terms as 'fusion' had in musical terms.

The start of the 90s demanded a process of serious consolidation, supportive funding and a great deal of analysis and self-examination. The issues had been clearly written on the wall by the dancers themselves. On the one hand, they were aesthetic: the nature of integrity in Indian dance; the precise character of innovation; the limits to collaboration across cultural divides. On the other, they were political, touching on ways in which work of different cultures was regarded by funding bodies and the devices they set in place to support it. Having been born in buoyantly on the shoulders of a campaigning spirit in the 1970s, the dance form ran the double danger facing many dissidents: of being either absorbed or falling out of fashion.

The 1990s provided dancers and choreographers with a harder agenda than many would have thought possible ten years before. But they had also, in the process, acquired some of the skills and sophistication necessary to deal with it.

Choreography and Dance, 1997, Vol 4(2), pp. 31–34
Reprints available directly from the publisher
Photocopying permitted by license only

© 1997 OPA (Overseas Publishers Association)
Amsterdam B.V. Published in The Netherlands
by Harwood Academic Publishers
Printed in India

Text Context Dance

Shobana Jeyasingh

"If history makes complexities let us not try to simplify them" Salman
Rushdie

– Imaginary Homelands

"The truest eye may now belong to the migrants' double vision" Homi
Baba

– The Location of Culture

In a recent lavish series on dance which was broadcast on British television, a
Bharata Natyam dancer from Madras was interviewed. Although the Madras
traffic could be heard in the no doubt carefully prepared soundtrack, the camera
cut to a rice field (nowhere near the offices and light industry of Madras) and
came to rest happily on a water droplet falling gently from a fresh green stem. The
background talk was of gods, goddesses and spiritual pursuits; it had to be since
the producers (not Indian) had already decided that Bharata Natyam was to come
under the heading of 'religion'. This was despite the fact that it is performed in
theatres not only in Madras but in major cities all over the world. Those interesting complications of history as the fact that the Bharata Natyam dancer, so exoti-
cally designed into the frame, spoke impeccable English and probably had a degree in computer science or that this "pure and religious" art form thrived within
a traffic invested city, were ignored. The fiction of "the Orient", so beloved in the
West as a place of simple spiritual certainties, exotic maidens and colourful ritu-
als, had to be reinforced once again to the viewers in their sitting rooms in London
and New York. There is simply no room for the realities of carbon monoxide in a
romance.

This stifling, historically inaccurate and ultimately life denying concept of the
East is not an isolated example. It is very much a symptom of a more general,
unequal power relationship between East and West. The West is the eternal anthropologist with the resources to observe, research and 'explain' all those exotic
cultures. It is a kind of colonisation through categorization and as such an exercise
of power. There are not many programmes on Indian television about the natives
of Tunbridge Wells but numerous ones on British television on selected aspects of
Indian life. It is Columbus who 'discovers' America because his descendants have
the power to control the telling of the story.

The evaluation and understanding of South Asian dance is often hampered by
assumptions which are the by products of this inequality.

As a choreographer my work is described as an East West collaboration because
I work with composers who are not Indian. The fact that we both share a common
British culture is never highlighted. The assumption is that "East", myself, must

be a simple, unchanging essence which stands for tradition and the Past and "West", the composer, represents change, modernity and dynamism. It is also symptomatic that when the "unchanging East" is influenced by the "West" it is always news. However, when the "West" is influenced by Indian musical structure (as is Philip Glass) or by African art (as was Picasso) or South Asian dance (as Martha Graham was), it is hardly something to comment upon or acknowledge. One very rarely hears of a West/East collaboration.

This polarised and inaccurate view of other cultures is barely understandable in previous centuries when geographical borders defined cultural identities and there was little chance to test one's ideas of other cultures in practice. The "India" that is the backdrop for a ballet like La Bayadère, with its kitsch orientalism and characters who could be anywhere from Cairo to Tokyo, is irksome to an Indian but understandable as a product of its time. It is less understandable to subscribe to such a landscape in the late twentieth century when the post colonial migration of peoples all over the globe has resulted in a blurring of a simple East and West divide especially as a cultural reference point. Migrations have occurred not only from the so-called third world to Europe and America, but from Britain to Australia and within Europe itself. Even within political and national boundaries people have moved from rural, provincial settings to ever increasing urban ones. One of the features of this century is that very few people live their lives like their parents and grandparents lived. The revolution in communications has further meant that people have set up global communities of common interest, whether it be of high finance or of personal predilections.

One such global community is the Indian diaspora which stretches from Fiji to Canada. The culture pertinent to it is characterised by a balancing act between old and new, memory and present day reality. The members of this diverse community live their lives in a cultural roundabout where many histories meet. A continuous stream of new arrivals at differing stages of acclimatisation make sure that nothing stays fixed for long. The choice concerning what road to take – preservation, innovation, community, mainstream, integration, seclusion or a mix of any of these possibilities – remans a purely individual one. The culture of the roundabout is historically new terrain and its landscape is just beginning to be charted. One can glimpse it in the multiple reference points in a Rushdie novel and in the tragicomedy of films like Bhaji and the Beach. The sculptures of Anish Kapoor in their very transcendence of cultural specifics declare themselves as a product of the roundabout, as does the rap music of Apache Indian. The culture of the diaspora challenges inherited ideas of home as something defined by geography. More and more "home" is becoming a radical and dynamic invention that is more about the future than the past, the sum of new journeys rather than the station that one has left behind.

It was my personal experience of homemaking that prompted me to choreograph one of my earliest dance works Making of Maps. As the title suggests it was not the end product but the process that I was interested in. I wanted to challenge the total inaccuracy of the "home ground" that was prescribed for me. I had spent my childhood and youth in four different countries and my artistic heritage was therefore diverse. The one thing that connected all the strands was the fact that I had always been a city dweller and felt at home in that particular pacing of life. The score for Making of Maps was therefore made up of the sounds

Figure 12 Shobana Jeyasingh Dance Company. Savitha Shekhar in *Making of Maps*. Photo: Chris Nash, 1993.

of a city: the hum of a conversation, traffic, railway stations; as well as domestic sounds. This was composed by Alistair MacDonald from Birmingham. Woven into the composition were fragments of a Carnatic music ensemble rehearsing, an ensemble put together by Ramamani who lives in Bangalore, South India. The music she composed for the piece emerged as a quote within the overall composition. It had the accessible entrance that the age of electronics has given to all types of music. At the press of a button, anywhere in the world either through the radio or through a music centre, the intimacy of a performance envelops the listener, while its separateness from one's surroundings is acknowledged. In fact, the way one can twiddle the knob of a radio and travel through diverse soundscapes was a metaphor that was used in the creation of the music. The manner in which MacDonald's music related to Ramamani's was important. The Indian music was not designed to be a dislocated or nostalgic episode and neither were the city sounds a negative and threatening force. In terms of dance language, our starting point was Bharata Natyam which was a given like race or gender. Just as the sounds that accompanied the dance moved from personal to formal the dance was influenced by purely personal concerns of vocabulary and composition.

Traditionally Bharata Natyam has a close affinity to the floor and the pull of gravity. The body "sits" in a demi plie position and energises itself through rhythmic contact between feet and ground. I wanted to push this affinity to its logical conclusion and had my dancers travel through demi plie, slide on to the floor and roll over. This embrace of the floor signalled a loosening of the prescribed "poise" that is part of the etiquette of the dance. This in turn made it easier to question, however tentatively, the self sufficiency of the Bharata Natyam body conditioned by its history as a solo art form. It was not just a matter of introducing touch and with it the implication of human emotion and relationships, but also the acceptance of physical dependency and trust. If the dance were to continue dancers had to be helped off the floor and pushed to the ground or helped to jump further. It was important that these interactions were casual as well as stylised.

MacDonald had engineered an extremely organic entry into and exit out of the Indian music. I did not want the dance language to change dramatically when we danced to Ramamani's music; that would have made that section seem either like a romantic and exotic interlude or made it more "real" than the city sounds. Therefore, whatever discoveries we had made in terms of vocabulary and composition were common to both. The changes in the dance in terms of density of structure or speed were in response to the differing musical structures rather than any perceived cultural changes. Carnatic music composition by its very nature dictates the ebb and flow of movement. MacDonald's music by contrast afforded the movement the freedom to breathe and find its own pacing.

It seemed fitting that *Making of Maps* should end with the sounds of the city. Usually these are used to evoke fragmentation, dissonance and disturbance. However, I personally have no negative feelings about living in London and neither do I feel that the sense of order which I find appealing in Bharata Natyam is undermined by it. The music takes the dance into a time and a place in the city when the sounds are gentler and more distant and where its diverse sounds weave a quiet and personal harmony of their own.

Choreography and Dance, 1997, Vol 4(2), pp. 35–38
Reprints available directly from the publisher
Photocopying permitted by license only

Maargam

Valli Subbiah

Maargam means 'path' and is a term used in Bharata Natyam to describe a particular sequence of dance items (dance pieces). A *maargam* reflects a conceptual voyage through sound, space and time. The music and dance vary in tempo, duration and content. A typical *maargam* format proceeds from *alarippu* to *tillana*.

The literal translation of *alarippu* is 'blossoming'. In dance terms there is a slow and steady build up from small movements of the eyes, neck and shoulders to deep bends and whole body movements, thus providing an ideal warm up for dancers, musicians and audience.

Jatiswaram which follows is musically a simple piece, with only the musical notes or swaras sung. Rhythmic dance or *nrtta* patterns are woven together highlighting the shape and structure of the form.

Abhinaya or expression is introduced for the first time in a *Sabdam*. The word to word meaning of the lyrics is expressed in a very literal way.

The main piece of a *maargam* is the *varnam*. The *varnam* allows for extensive development of *abhinaya* and *nrtta*, both structurally and conceptually. The *varnam* challenges the dancer and the musician to a dialogue and to develop the fine art of improvisation. It is a difficult and demanding piece to perform in which the dancers stamina, expertise and creativity are tested.

A series of *abhinaya* pieces is presented in the second half of a *maargam*. More liberties are taken by the dancer who moves away from the taught sequences and develops his or her own personal way. The audience gets a glimpse or the essence of the dancer and musician in these pieces.

The *tillana* is the culmination of the *maargam*. Like the *jatiswaram*, the focus is on *nrtta*, but is much more rhythmitically intricate. It is aptly referred to as a dance of joy.

Originally a form of worship, Bharata Natyam gradually shifted to the status of secular art form. The present *maargam* format was devised in the mid 19th century by Vadivelu who hailed from a family of musicians in Tanjore, South India. Vadivelu was also responsible for introducing the western violin to the Carnatic music style. The music used for the various pieces of the *maargam* span a creative period of three centuries. Some of the very beautiful, slow, expressional pieces date from the 17th century.

Over the years Bharata Natyam, along with all other Indian art forms has opened its door to many influences of the time: cultural, religious, political or social which enabled it to grow and evolve. This is reflected in the way the *maargam* expanded. Interrelated art forms like literature and music, which have always been a source of inspiration, began to play a much larger role in the development of the *maargam*. Political changes affected the development of dance in India. When the centre of political and social happenings shifted from the temple to the royal courts, so did

Figure 13   Valli Subbiah. Courtesy of Valli Subbiah.

the dance. When royal patronage began to decline, art forms, especially dance, suffered. By the end of the last century dance was looked upon by the imperialist rulers and many upper class Indians as an immoral art form. Eventually the practice or performance was banned.

It was a period in which there was no growth or development in the world of Indian dance. A gap of about fifty years made efforts to revive what was lost a very difficult task. People like Rukmini Devi and Ram Gopal had to travel from village to village hunting out teachers and begging them to teach. Evidence from sculpture and literature as well as from a dying breed of dance teachers or gurus was used to reconstruct the dances and put them into a context relevant to the times. Careful consideration was required to bring back the dignity and stature the dance form deserved.

Maargam in Training and Performance

In order to discuss *maargam* in training and performance in depth it is important to look at the basic concepts of Bharata Natyam and its relevance today. When learning or teaching any language both the grammatical and communicative aspects are essential for writing prose and poetry. Similarly, in the language of Bharata Natyam, both *nrtta* and *abhinaya* are essential tools for a student.

In Britain there is a sense of awareness and a growing interest in the *nrtta* aspect of Bharata Natyam. Whilst this is very positive, equal emphasis must be placed on the *abhinaya* aspect. *Nrtta* and *abhinaya* cannot be viewed in isolation. Any classical art strives for an equal and proportionate distribution of form and sentiment. The distinction in Bharata Natyam between these two concepts form as pure technical movement and sentiment as expressional dance, is abundantly apparent; and this distinction is the inner dynamics of the style.

On another level sharing and blending of concepts East to West, ancient to modern, among all forms of art is important but it is equally important to understand and retain the individual flavour of each art form. Once a student has learnt the basics of footwork and body movement, the use of hand gestures or *mudra-s*, further technical as well as aesthetic development leads to the learning of the *maargam*. The process of learning dance items is as integral a part as mastering the basic dance alphabet.

Subtle movements of the body or face are not taught as separate units of movement but as part of a whole. In a *nrtta* sequence a sliding movement of the feet would be accompanied by a certain tilt of the head or use of tiny neck movements (*attami*) or a particular glance; the movement of a dancer enacting a character covering her face with the pallu of her saree and then looking through it to observe something in the distance, cannot be broken down into separate movements. The physical movement is layered with a particular portrayal of a character with all its subtle shades of expression. The technique of improvisation comes with being able to elaborate a single word into an entire story, a strand of thought into an entire concept. This wealth of knowledge must not be lost; we must take advantage of what comes through a *maargam*.

Since I am a performer and teacher in Britain, the question of relevance is often posed to me. Can a dancer relate to a character outside his/her own experience? Can women walking with pots on their head or a Radha feeling dejected that

Krishna has not come, be portrayed?

It is important to move away from this narrow outlook. To be part of Indian dance you must be part of theatre. The theatricality of Indian dance is similar to theatricality anywhere in the world. *Abhinaya* is a skill: it is a part of the learning experience of an actor. Every role an actor portrays s not always a reflection of that actor's life.

An artist goes beyond the term 'Radha', is inspired by the music, the poetry, the choreography and is able to transcend names. The goal of *abhinaya* is not a literal rendition of mythological archetypes. In practical terms, a simple line of poetry is only the seed for the dancer. From it s/he must cultivate an ever growing flow of images which come from tradition but are not necessarily bound by it.

In a multicultural society like Britain there is ample room for classical as well as modern work. If classical work is overshadowed by an all encompassing focus of choreography as a reflection of the 'moment', then both types of work will suffer. We do not need boundaries and restrictions governed by our environment. What we need is to look towards expansion. Expansion in the classical idiom could very well mean a retrograde voyage, an enrichment of expressive possibilities by drawing on traditional techniques.

The important element about poetry in dance is not story or character as such, but the emotion that they embody which the poet tries to communicate. The source of inspiration for Indian dance, which has been the Hindu concept of life, serves as an enhancer not a detractor, widens not narrows, includes not excludes, any particular group of people. It is essential that we as performers and teachers keep this in mind.

A superficial understanding of Indian dance may lead to the belief that by eliminating *abhinaya* the link with religion is severed. Indian dance is made up of several layers: every line, triangle, square or circle within the *nrtta* aspect as well as every *mudra* and movement in *abhinaya* can be attributed to some form or another of religious thought or ritual.

Indian dance must be viewed as a whole, not in fragmented pieces. Why repeat mistakes of the past and cast away precious seeds of knowledge only to try to revive it thirty years hence?

To ensure growth and continuity of this art form, students and audience must not be deprived of knowledge or a variety of experiences. Instead, we must take advantage of living in Britain and give them that multiplicity of choice.

Choreography and Dance, 1997, Vol 4(2), pp. 39–43
Reprints available directly from the publisher
Photocopying permitted by license only

Teaching and Choreographing Kathak Dance in Britain

Nilima Devi

Before writing about my experience as a choreographer, dancer and teacher of Kathak living in Britain and assessing the position of Kathak dance today, it may be relevant to give a brief introduction to my Indian dance background. We shall then consider developments in Britain and the exciting prospects for new choreographic work.

Figure 14   Nilima Devi. Courtesy of Nilima Devi.

Indian Foundations

My interest in dance arose in childhood; formal training in Kathak began at the age of 13. I took my Diploma, B. Mus. and M. Mus. at the Faculty of Performing Arts in Baroda Music College. Already as students, some of us were involved in solo performances and I also took part in Kathak ballets. This developed some awareness of the differences between dance choreography as a soloist and group work.

After the Master, I began to prepare students for dance exams, but after one year I got married and went to Germany. I found that audiences there appreciated my interpretation of Kathak stories, especially the drama of Shakuntala. It was obvious that audiences enjoyed following the Kathak way of story telling through dance. Teaching Kathak in several cities was an interesting experience in interaction with foreign cultures, mainly with German students.

I moved to Leicester in 1980 and discovered to my dismay that even Asians knew very little about Indian dance forms. There were also virtually no facilities for learning Indian classical dance. Having founded the Institute of Classical Indian Dance, on 1st January 1981 I began classes. I started with three students but later hundreds came and went. Some found it too difficult; others thought they would learn and be able to perform Kathak within a few days. Once the initial hunger for the new dance experience was satisfied, only few dedicated souls continued regular training. The introduction of a structured syllabus for a six-year diploma course in Kathak has encouraged students to aim towards a formal qualification; six students have completed our diploma course.

Branching Out in Britain

My Indian experience of teaching for exams also helped to build up a structured training programme for Kathak dance, starting with auditions for children from seven years old onwards with weekly classes in several centres. This has now become an important part of Leicestershire's pioneering dance provisions under the umbrella of Asian Youth Dance.

Apart from weekly technical Kathak training, there are special performance-related training programmes which involve a lot of new choreographic work. There is constant demand for small and large presentations of dance groups. We now have a well organised system of presenting annual showcase performances of Indian music and dance, which regularly attract capacity audiences. This puts a lot of pressure on the skills of choreographers and dancers.

Whether I am working as an Asian Dance Animateur, as a dancer who goes into schools and gives lecture-demonstrations and 'taster sessions', as a teacher within the mainstream education system, or in a formal stage setting, choreographic skills are always in demand, at different levels and for quite different purposes.

The Joys of Choreography

Through performing and teaching, I found again and again that Kathak stories are very well received. No matter what some people say about the lack of relationship of traditional Indian dance to life in Britain, such stories have become an important educational vehicle for multicultural teaching in British schools.

However, this is not the goal of choreographic development for a Kathak dancer in Britain today. Having encouraged and presented many Kathak students in performance work, I have begun to enjoy working on group choreography for them. This was my British beginning of choreography and dance, I am planning to do much more such work as part of my teaching. At the same time, I continue to enjoy the challenge of devising dance pieces for myself. I cannot make sense of the official division of South Asian dancers into traditional and contemporary categories. For me, these are artificial definitions which break down in the studio, whether I use traditional Kathak music or a totally different score, even European music. Working on a traditional repertoire piece in a new setting or in a new form is very much a creative process and I do not see that a dance form like Kathak is ever stagnant and static.

In Germany I choreographed a seven minute piece of Kathak dance to Beethoven's Piano Concerto n.1. The inspiration for this developed when I was expecting my first child. I used to listen to all kinds of music. One day, in the midst of listening to Beethoven's Piano Concerto, I threw away my knitting and started dancing. Working on the finer points of the choreography had to wait until after delivery! Later, when preparing for performances in India, I decided to take something new from Europe and re-choreographed this piece for a larger stage. It was certainly not easy, because the music was so different and I was a bit reluctant at first to cross the traditional Kathak boundaries. Emphasising the rhythmic patterns helped to choreograph a piece which people in India really like but audiences here found strange. As one student said, "Indian dance needs Indian music".

By 1986 as some of my students had developed their skills, I began to re-choreograph some 'traditional' solo Kathak dance pieces into group works. These dances from the technical Kathak repertoire proved particularly effective and it was enjoyable to experience with different movement patterns and rhythmic synchronisation. In 1987 we presented an *Evening of Indian Dance* showcase in which various ability and age groups from schools and communities were involved. This was challenging in terms of setting up complex dance pieces based on Kathak for students who were training in Kathak, synchronised with folk and creative movements for children who had never performed before. It was certainly enjoyable to see the end result.

As the group of students trained in Kathak became more aware of the use of space and acquired more technical proficiency, we began to explore whole stories, for which obviously group choreography would be needed. In 1988, *Seasons of India* again brought together different ability groups from schools and community centres as well as Kathak students. In the process, more sophisticated use of various objects such as backdrops, varied colour lighting, dance costumes and other material developed. The 1989 production of *The Ugly Duckling* a dance ballet set to a creative score of Indian music, involved combining solo pieces for the main characters with mass scenes of farmyard animals and a delightful flock of beautiful swans in the finale dance. This Kathak ballet became so popular that it was reproduced, with different casting, in 1992/93 and will probably be re-choreographed in the future.

The creative process of producing this kind of ballet was a challenging multi-level experience. Having prepared a script from the fairy tale, we identified which scenes would need to be choreographed and a music score was created by composers who knew Kathak dance and could base some parts of their score on familiar rhythmic patterns. The end result was an ear-catching tune which inspired

Figure 15   Nilima Devia and students, Kathak. Courtesy of Nilima Devi.

everybody to enjoy the play. It had rhythms and quite unusual choreography for a Kathak dance piece. How do you show a freezing duckling in Kathak style? And how do you depict the hatching of four sweet little ducklings and an ugly one? Almost all barriers of tradition and modernity were crossed in this menagerie. In its first version, more than 50 school children took part, while the major roles were taken by some advanced Kathak students. For touring this production, the mass scenes of the farmyard had to be re-choreographed but the rest could actually stay almost as it was.

This production was followed by *The Triangle*, set up for myself and two of my senior students. Initially we toured with live music, using a combination of Eastern and Western drumming, and created a melée of various dance pieces: a train journey; kite flying spring festival scenes; invoking blessings; interspersed with a lot of rhythmic mathematics. It was a new experience to put together a variety of creative small pieces, loosely connected by a contemporary theme but focused on Indian images. Not surprisingly, Indian audiences found this delightful because it was familiar, whereas the joys of cutting other people's kites and the intricacies of Ganesha's beauty might escape other audiences. This shows that some extra effort may indeed be needed to make one's creations understood, but as a Kathak dancer I am obviously familiar with the notion that an audience may just sit back and enjoy the movement aspects or the rhythmic intricacies of a performance.

More recently, my choreographic work with Kumudini Lakhia, who directed our new production *Rainbow* based on the abstract philosophy of the *Bhagavadgītā*, has given me further insights into choreographic techniques.

Currently, the biggest challenge in the development of South Asian dance choreography is putting together groups of different standards to create effective stage presentations. Since 1988, every year the performance season has brought forth new Indian dance work, based on Kathak, folk and creative dance movements and involving music scores from solo tabla to orchestral music and American Indian chanting. South Asian dance and its choreographic development has become part of Britain's multicultural experience and demands of practitioners that they think creatively and present their dance form in all kinds of ways. If there is world music, so we must have world dance too. Whether regional and national funding bodies are aware of this or not, in Britain today there is a lively South Asian 'dance scene' which involves much more input from choreography than the so-called 'experts' are willing to see.

Choreography and Dance, 1997, Vol 4(2), pp. 45–49
Reprints available directly from the publisher
Photocopying permitted by license only

Choreographing *Delicious Arbour*: Richard Alston in Conversation with Vena Gheerawo, June 1995

Vena Gheerawo

Richard Alston was one of the original students at the London School of Contemporary Dance School, beginning his career as choreographer back in 1968. He later studied with Merce Cunningham and then worked principally as an independent choreographer throughout Europe. He was made Resident Choreographer with Ballet Rambert in 1980 and later became Rambert's Artistic director. He left Rambert in 1992 and choreographed a number of works for various companies, among which was the Shobana Jeyasingh Company. The piece Alston choreographed for Shobana's dancers, *Delicious Arbour* set to Purcell's music, made use of the Bharata Natyam idiom in an experimental way and indeed broke new ground. Alston was subsequently made Artistic Director of the Contemporary Dance Trust, forming his own company with former members of the London Contemporary Dance Theatre (LCDT) in 1994. Here he talks to Vena Gheerawo about *Delicious Arbour* and what it was like to work with a form, a 'language' as he likes calling it, which was fundamentally alien and yet so close to him at a deep level in that it reflected his sense of classicism.

Shobana approached me to choreograph a piece. She could see that I worked with a formal language, a kind of classical vocabulary. That is why she was interested in seeing what I could do if I worked with Bharata Natyam dancers. Shobana is a very interesting person, someone whom I really respect. I responded to her interest. So we did workshops for one year. They were very important workshops because they taught me a lot about what would not work; the workshops were not very successful. At the end of it I was quite worried whether I should do it or not. I became cautious. Then I found that this was the only project I had, following a drastic change in my professional circumstances. So, there were really practical motivations. I was quite scared and tried to make sure that I would do it to the best of my abilities. I felt it was one of the most courageous things I ever found myself doing. In the end I got so much from it, it probably was a much happier experience than I originally thought it could be. What I think I have as a human being is a sense of very deep joy in dancing; it really makes me feel alive. It is always there and is my real motivation, for all my work: to get that sense of joy and enjoyment.

What worried me was the fact that it is possible with such a formal language to be very proficient within that language and yet make dancers look awkward by taking them beyond what they can do. It seems to me that the language of Bharata Natyam is ultimately based on a very deep bending of the joints, rather than long extended lines. So extended movements are something very alien to someone who has been trained in this very set language with different physical properties. I have seen that happen with other people, have seen very proficient Western dancers make very proficient Kathak or Bharata Natyam dancers look extremely awkward because they have not really understood the language.

For me the penny dropped because I am very interested in rhythmic phrases. That provided a link. Also, in contemporary dance, to a more limited extent, of course, in comparison with Bharata Natyam, we work with our weight onto the floor. So, I would start with some sort of rhythm in the feet, some sense of the weight being down. Then I would phrase it in my way, which is sort of up and down. Bharata Natyam is a solo form and makes space in the central axis which is not quite natural. At least, this is the way I understand it. So it was quite interesting to try and find ways to travel. My work is very much about travelling, from here to there. I found it to be one of the most interesting problems, one which became increasingly interesting as the project went along: getting people to jump and move in a way that would eventually become comfortable even if it was not when we first tried it. I would get them to do things they were not used to sensitively enough, in a way that would not cause injury. It is interesting that these women – two of them are actually living in England, but the others came from Bangalore and Madras – are from a climate that is warm and makes the muscles relax. We started working in September and we tried to look after these people. Shobana would address that too by giving them warm up exercises and yoga so that they actually learnt about preparing themselves in a different climate. What is that very slow form of martial art called? *Kalari Payaṭṭu*, yes, that is what they were doing. They were finding a way of warming up that was very relevant for them. They worked with someone who does body conditioning. Shobana told me that in a hot climate classes would be in the early evening. It is a totally different physical feeling.

So Shobana approached me, not so much to see whether we had a common language but mainly to find ways to help her put Bharata Natyam in a new context. This is what she is doing; she is living here and working here. She is passionately committed to the Bharata Natyam language and its rich vocabulary and she wanted to see what would happen if choreographers from the culture she is trying to work in looked at this language.

I learnt a lot about myself while doing this work, putting myself in a different place. There I was, a Western male choreographer, interacting with a group of women who had worked in a situation which was traditional, with a guru. My creative juices flow when everyone is at ease. I am talking about social things. These women had a terrific sense of humour. I definitely wanted to remove myself from a sort of pseudo guru position and this happened easily, with great laughter and enjoyment. They gave me a lot. Shobana had chosen very well. She had chosen people who were not just talented but also excited about working in a different way, which could be very exposing. The workshops I had done the year before had been with a different group who were much more withdrawn. These young women gave a lot and we had lots of time, which was very important.

I was basically ignorant about Bharata Natyam. I had seen performances but I had no idea how people were trained. In the early stages I felt that I needed to understand what this language was by seeing as much as possible. So everyday I would say "Right, now I would like to see, I would like you to show me something". And what astonished me was that Shobana would say "Right, show him. . . ." usually very, very short things and some sort of rhythmic theme. They showed me *alarippu* and I began to get a sense of how they learnt movement and how they felt about movement. The other thing that was tremendously important was the Purcell. If I had chosen something which was very melodic it would have been much harder. I discovered that they had a tremendously strong sense of rhythm but, quite understandably, no sense of the western *rubato*. When we were working with a recording if the string orchestra slowed down, these young women would not . . . Shobana explained that within the rules of Indian music to slow down is absolutely wrong. It was fascinating to see that sometimes they could not hear the rubato. They would depart, keeping absolutely within their own rhythmic phrases and then they would be astonished to see that they had finished and the music was still there . . . Still, Purcell's rhythm is very robust and as he wrote in the 17th century he used asymmetrical phrases. Of course, they were nothing like the complexities of Asian music, but it became a very good way of meeting because the dancers enjoyed the music a lot.

I did not really know what to do: I was listening to all sorts of music. I thought there was no point in imitating Shobana who uses contemporary composers. I love Purcell: I have lots of records of Purcell. I am ashamed really to say how trivially the choice was made. I saw a record called Indian Queen and I thought it might be relevant. I listened to it, then really felt that Purcell was right for this. His music has a marvellous sense of weight. I mostly work with twentieth century music but not always, so this was not an absolute departure. Once the music was found, I felt a marvellous sense of release. I had been quite anxious. And even if the work situation had been more difficult, this music gave me such pleasure that it would have kept my spirits up, even if I had found it hard to find the right language to carry it. In the end there were none of these problems. It is important to have music that gives you a lot of joy; that joy seems to transcend cultures.

I have always found it exciting that dance and music can come together through rhythm. Rhythmic phrases are something that have interested me, since my student days. Because I sometimes like to make phrases with very fast steps, when I teach I make a lot of noises expressing the rhythmic phrase. Voicing the rhythmic phrases is my personal way to link the dance and the music. I discovered I could do that with those dancers and it has given me a tool in the way I teach now.

I certainly enjoyed this work. It is perhaps now a question of time – I have my own company – but I do not think of it as a once only thing. What I did was nothing compared to what Shobana is doing now, but I do think that having someone else coming into her work space was very liberating for her. I felt that her work, the work she did at the same time, *Romance with Footnotes*, was a big step forward, for her. It is sometimes tremendously revealing to see your dancers work with someone else. Geographically she is very far from her roots and so in a certain sense she has worked in a pioneering way. It must be quite lonely. So we would talk and share things. *Romance with Footnotes* took her in a new direction. I thought the language was really outstanding. In comparison, the Purcell piece is naive, which is understandable, as it was an experiment.

It is very interesting to take on a project which you want to treat with respect. You do not want the artistic equivalent of colonialising, of grabbing and using. I did not deal with this, in a sense I sidestepped it. The Purcell music is very baroque and has a connection with gods and heroes. Bharata Natyam is traditionally associated with gods and heroes so the elaborate and very expressive use of the arm made a link with the baroque music. I remember someone, an English-man, not a dancer, who had come to one of the rehearsals, said "Oh, it is fascinat-ing how you put together the baroque arms with the Indian footwork". And of course I had not! The only thing that I changed was that I did not want every movement to be repeated on the other side, in the typical way of Bharata Natyam. They were wonderful young dancers, especially Savita and Verni. I do not think people would have worked so well if they had not enjoyed it.

·If I were asked again, I would be glad to do another work. It was only a way to say hello, really.

I feel that, as a result of that experience I now tend to work in greater detail. What I was constantly asked was "And how do you want the hands?". You can train for years as a classical ballet dancer and never think of the hands as not being part of a line. You would not focus on them specifically. But here it was part of the language. At the time an uninformed journalist asked me "And will you now use *mudra-s* in your own choreography after this experience?" Of course not; that would be trivial. This whole experience made me aware of the fact that I can and do think in detail. Sometimes you do not use things that you can actually do. What I learnt from it was that Bharata Natyam is a very rich, detailed, mature language and, in its traditional form, its purpose is very clear. Looking in detail at any language like that is enriching but to copy, to get my dancers to do things clearly taken out of this language would be nothing but trivialising it. On mondays we have Bharata Natyam classes here at The Place and the dancers get to bend their knees really well. To me that is not as fruitful.

I often thought that Bharata Natyam was incredibly like classical ballet. In classical ballet you can say to dancers "Show me *chassé* or *pas de chat*, whatever ", and they will show it. It is exactly the same in Bharata Natyam. I was able to work quickly because I could "steal" phrases. I would say "Show me" and then "Oh, we could do this." There is a lovely jump, a travelling step with change of the arms. I would use it a lot and it would remind me of classical ballet. Classical ballet and Bharata Natyam share an origin as a proscenium art. My sense of classical ballet was what took me through. It made a direct link. Probably it would be quite hard to find classical dancers who would really be open to work-ing in this manner.

That is why I really liked these dancers; they were open. Shobana gave marvel-lous support. We tried some things which were very hard, but I never let them do anything that was too uncomfortable. I was interested to see the way things changed, how they became comfortable, especially for Verni, who suddenly began to travel and did a huge circle in the solo. I felt by the end of the project I knew a lot more about Bharata Natyam although still at a very basic level, I knew more about that language and therefore I knew more about dancing.

When I choreograph, I start with music. It is a strong instinct in me. I feel that I would really like to see somebody moving with the music. I like working with contemporary music and I find it exciting if someone says to me "Oh I do not usually care for contemporary music but watching what you did with that piece I found it quite exciting". I think that it was this sense of sharing the concept of dance as visualisation of music that helped me to find a common ground. This is the way dance is traditionally perceived in India and this is the way I see dance.

Would I do it again? Yes. It is not so much about what Bharata Natyam and I can give to each other, it is about putting oneself in a strange place, which is a wonderful way of learning. However, now I need to step back rather than rushing into it. I need to distance myself, then, perhaps, look again at the video. Then I will be able to talk about it with greater detachment. But I certainly have no regrets.

Choreography and Dance, 1997, Vol 4(2), pp. 51–53
Reprints available directly from the publisher
Photocopying permitted by license only

© 1997 OPA (Overseas Publishers Association)
Amsterdam B.V. Published in The Netherlands
by Harwood Academic Publishers
Printed in India

South Asian Dance: The British Experience? Holism and Individualism

Vena Gheerawo

I am not convinced that there is a British experience of South Asian dance, if by that one means the way British people perceive South Asian dance. I am a dancer of Indian descent and British by birth and education. My upbringing has seen a combination of both 'Eastern' and 'Western' cultures; influences from both have moulded my being. I am very conscious of this, but the two have not remained separate as two different parts of my consciousness. They are intrinsically fused. I do not identify individually with two separate cultures. They are both part of my identity.

Figure 16   Vena Gheerawo. Courtesy of Vena Gheerawo.

I originally trained in London in Bharata Natyam; one of the most highly rec-
ognised styles of Indian classical dance. I made my debut solo concert under Shri
Prakash Yadagudde of the Institute of Indian Culture in 1990. My longing for greater
freedom of choreography, a wider range of movement and a deeper understanding of the dance tradition took me to India and to Dr Padma Subrahmanyam. Her
research on the *Nāṭyaśāstra*, the oldest extant text on Indian dramaturgy, led her
to reconstruction of the technique described therein. This is based on *karaṇa-s* (units
of dance) which allow an unparalleled variety of movement in contrast to the
contemporary classical dances prevalent in India today. Dr Subrahmanyam named
this long lost style Bharata Nrityam.

The training I received from her was rigorous and disciplined – far more disciplined than any of my previous learning experiences. I was seventeen and had
just completed my A levels[1] when I left for India. In the eyes of most of the people
I came across in Madras I was a British person coming into one of the most orthodox schools of dance in the country. How would I respond to the system which
places such emphasis on unquestioning reverence for the Guru (teacher)? It was
interesting to note people's surprise when I did not live up to their expectations
of a 'Westerner' with all the associations of decadence. Equally amusing were the
concerned cautions of a handful of well meaning 'Westerners' who were convinced
that my privileged English education had not prepared me to face the poverty of
a Third World country. I had to make a conscious decision not to expect anything
but simply go and experience. I cannot claim that my experience was a representative British one or even that it was typical of an Anglo-Indian. This would
deny individuality and the essentially human capacity to reason, to perceive anew,
to reinterpret according to one's awareness. More immediately, stereotypes have
proved to be misleading.

As my training in the Art has progressed it has increasingly become part of my
being. My body became more accustomed to the technique of dance, the outer
form; ongoing practice increased the aptitude for dance movements. But "Indian
dance transcends mere movement" as Dr Subrahmanyam says. The *bhāva* (inner
content) is of prime importance in the proper execution of dance. It is the emotion
which brings to life *nṛtta* (pure dance movement) and *abhinaya* (the mimetic aspect of dance). It is this that communicates to an audience, this that makes the
movement meaningful. The capacity to infuse the dance with this inner content
grows with time. The more I continue to dance, the greater the depth of my feeling
for it. And I do feel it, passionately and spontaneously.

But I do not feel it as an Indian or as a Briton but for itself. It involves the whole
of the individual. There is no separate Indian part of my psyche which connects
with things Indian and from which the rest is detached. I think that such a partial
involvement would produce partial results. It would be possible to live like this,
to assume a new persona for a new situation and deny the identity of the previous
moment. I have seen this done, but the result is superficiality, denial and loss of
identity.

The concept of *bhāva* puts the emphasis on individuality. This cannot be super-
imposed from without by a teacher; it must come from within. The nature of each
dancer feeds her dance and is received by the audience. This allows scope for the

---

[1]   General Certificate of Education, Advanced Level.

expression of the individual, however much the technique may be fixed. This is especially true of *nṛtta*, in which there is no given meaning to the movement, so the manner of presentation is left to the dancer. This individualism is suffused with holism in that it involves the whole person: body, mind, heart and spirit. This apparent paradox is reflected in the communicative capacity of the dance.

It is important to retain the integrity of Bharata Nrityam; this includes acknowledging that it is an Indian form of dance based on specifically Indian spiritual concepts, religious ideas and aesthetic principles. I have been steeped in Indian mythology and ideology and my devotion to the Art and the divinity from which it claims origin springs from my involvement in that. However, this aspect of the individuality of the Art, its peculiarly Indian basis, does not limit it to an Indian audience. Again, individuality does not deny holism and is not opposed to it.

The majority of my audiences are non-Indian, mainly British, a fact which speaks for itself. I have often heard the phrase 'to preserve Indian culture abroad' repeated in connection with second generation Indians in Britain taking an active interest in learning the music and dance of India. But there is much more to be done than the mere preservation of a self-contained heritage. Presenting Bharata Nrityam to international audiences represents the progress and growth of artistry – growth because it is being enjoyed and lived by more people. The format of my presentation is as follows. If the audience is a new one, with no prior knowledge of Indian dance, I briefly introduce the form and its ethos. I always precede each piece with an introduction explaining its contents. If it is an item of *abhinaya* (relating a story or theme) I narrate the gist of the story demonstrating the corresponding gestures that will be used in the dance. This enables the audience to follow the mime more easily, making the dance accessible and meaningful.

Here is the response of one member of an audience, a recruitment consultant from London who had very little prior knowledge of South Asian dance: "That was beautiful. Knowing very little my enjoyment arose from the art, poise and drama. I appreciate the beauty of the songs even though I do not understand the words. Stories without words, in movement which is universal. Watching the emotion of the dancer and having that transferred to myself – the feeling wrapped and tossed me. The rhythm of the dancer's body, the music and song all seemed to combine as one. It was a total experience".

The extent of his involvement is evident. Clearly, responses will vary from person to person, but it does seem that the Art speaks to the individual, spilling over imposed divisions such as nationality. Beauty, emotion, movement are universal; however much the genre is specific, these shine through as universal.

The point about the unknown language not being an inhibition struck a chord with me. In my early years of training my teacher would painstakingly explain the song word by word as he taught me. I was ignorant of any Indian language. The study of Sanskrit and a year in Madras with Tamil speakers have given me some understanding of these two languages, but there is still much that I have translated for myself into English so that I can feel and express what the song says. Thus my own understanding is through a second language, yet this has not proved to be a great inhibition to my connection with the Art, or apparently the audience's appreciation of it. This questions the importance that is usually attached to understanding a language as a means to the associated culture. The essence of dance goes beyond words.

Choreography and Dance, 1997, Vol 4(2), pp. 55–62
Reprints available directly from the publisher
Photocopying permitted by license only

Dance, South Asian Dance, and Higher Education

Andrée Grau

Introduction

A piece on South Asian dance and Higher Education could be approached in a number of ways. One could, for instance, start by arguing that dance in general, let alone South Asian, is hardly significant in contemporary British society and barely established at university level. One could then continue by presenting a survey of all the courses and workshops which incorporate South Asian dance in one form or another, and conclude that, although a great deal more still needs to be done, the achievements thus far should be celebrated. Such a piece might be a valuable documentation, but hardly visionary. My intention here is to raise broader issues which are significant for Dance Studies in general. Whilst this piece focuses on and takes its examples from British institutions, the issues it raises – eurocentrism and racism in particular – hold true for most dance departments concentrating on Western theatre dance around the world.

Dance scholars (myself included) have often bemoaned the lack of interest in dance by modern Western society in general and by academic institutions in particular. Nevertheless dance is currently being offered by almost 30 institutions of Higher Education throughout the UK. Although Peter Brinson's vision that 'dancers and dance people can be, should be, role models, ideal people and personalities for all the people of Britain to follow' (1994: 2) is unlikely to become a reality in the near future, standard statistical surveys have indicated unequivocally the prominent part some dance forms play in contemporary British cultural life. As many tickets, for example, are sold each week for dance halls and discos as for football matches and the cinema (Brinson 1991: 3), *Come dancing* is the longest running television series in Britain (Ward 1993: 17), and 'dance-style routines and movements are a feature of the highly populated adult 'aerobic' and 'step' classes which are held throughout the day, almost every day of the year, in leisure centres and fitness clubs throughout the country' (Thomas 1995: 2). Dance has definitely a place as a cultural product in this country.

'Dance' as a concept, however, is problematic since it has so many different manifestations and few dance departments could, or would be willing, to consider catering for them all. For most dance programmes in the UK, 'dance' is both Eurocentric and elitist, consisting primarily of what can be loosely described as 'Western theatre dance'. Within the constraints of such frameworks and structures, both in terms of philosophy and of organisation, South Asian dance is often marginalised.[1] Some dance educators, however, are gradually acknowledging that the dance cultures of other countries have much to give to British dance in terms of diversification of styles and larger movement vocabularies. The end of parochialism in dance has started becoming a reality and we see the beginning of 'the development of cultural diversity and understanding in our society so that British dance culture embraces today not just classical, contemporary and traditional folk dance forms but dance influences from Africa, the Caribbean, South Asia, China, South America and other cultures.' (Brinson 1994: 4). If the trend continues, South Asian dance forms will no longer be perceived by many mainstream dance workers and dancers as minority arts for minority groups.

South Asian Dance in Higher Education: Some Examples

Within the majority of institutions offering dance in this country, South Asian dancers can only be invited to contribute on an occasional basis. They give workshops, lecture-demonstrations, or seminars on both classical and folk forms originating from the Indian subcontinent, as well as on contemporary British developments of these forms. This is often done within the context of *Community Dance, Dance and Culture*, or *Dance in Society* options, as a way of illustrating broader sociological, political, historical and/or cultural issues. Only occasionally are they part of choreography or aesthetics courses. These contributions, although important, are far too irregular and ad hoc to discuss here.

A number of institutions also offer, or have offered modules on aspects of South Asian dance, usually an introduction to one or more classical styles, such as Kathak, Bharata Natyam, Odissi, and/or Kathakali, within their existing dance and performing arts course (for example at the Laban Centre, The London Contemporary Dance School, Surrey University, and Middlesex University). Such courses have positive and negative qualities and have often been labelled as mere tokens, included more for political correctness than intrinsic value.

Detractors can talk about the arrogant assumptions made by these contributions. How can students have any understanding of such highly complex forms after thirty to forty hours of practice/lectures when most of them knew next to nothing about them to start with? Why is it that within these courses students are often expected not only to learn about the dance forms themselves but also to look in some details at the broader socio-cultural framework? They have to learn about the cultural diversity of dance in the UK today as well as develop an appreciation of dance as an activity which has the potential to cross cultural boundaries. Can it be done? These are obviously crucial issues that must be looked at, but would the expectations be similar for a course in contemporary dance? How much do students studying, Graham technique for example, know about its original context, of its place within contemporary dance in general, of the context of its introduction in the UK and so on? Unless they have also taken a course in the history of contemporary dance, they know very little. Why assume then, that the information can be condensed for a South Asian technique and taught within a single module?

---

[1]   See, for example, Maree's comment in a previous issue of this journal, about South Asian dance not being 'another bump that's even more marginal than dance itself' (1992: 60).

Defendants, on the other hand, can argue that such courses open a window – and nobody pretends they can do more – onto one of the important areas of world dance. At least the options exist, they say, broadening the students' perspectives and sowing the seeds for a better level of South Asian dance provision in the UK. Looking at South Asian dance as art dances in their own right allows students to have some appreciation of dance styles outside the confines of Western theatre dance. Exploring a new vocabulary of movement, discovering muscles they never knew existed, helps students further develop their individual potential and awareness, bringing new creative energy and understanding to dance in general.

Clearly both side of the argument are valid and we are now at a point when decisions are being made by dance departments to channel South Asian dance in new directions where this kind of debate would one day, hopefully, become irrelevant. I will discuss here the paths taken by four institutions: Surrey University, Middlesex University, University College Bretton Hall, and the London Contemporary Dance School, since they represent significant trends.

One of the problems which comes to the surface when looking at South Asian Dance education and training in the UK, is that they depend almost entirely upon performers teaching. Practising dance artists are undoubtedly essential within dance departments, whether or not students are trained as performers or as people supporting the dance profession more generally. But as Shobhana Jeyasingh has argued 'if we draw comparison with contemporary dance it would be as though responsibility for producing all the contemporary dancers in Britain had to be taken by, say Siobhan Davies and Yolande Snaith' (Jeyasingh 1994: 57).

The needs of dance artists and of education, however, are not always synonymous. Performers frequently find educational structures constrictive. They are often ill-equipped with the skills to carry out the administrative tasks required of them and this is true of all performers, not just South Asian dancers! The difference, however, is that contemporary dance artists can, for instance, rely on a support network of teaching colleagues, knowledgeable about their art form. This is not necessarily true for their South Asian counterparts. Few, if any, dance departments can claim to have specialists on South Asian Dance as part of their full time faculty.

Furthermore dance artists, throughout the spectrum of styles, rarely conceive of their work as being part of a bigger conceptual framework. They often take on board the prejudices of their profession and their society. Reading about South Asian dancers' experiences in school, for example, I repeatedly found statements such as 'I teach folk and technique' taking technique to mean "classical", as if folk dance had no technique. This is exactly the attitude that Keali'inohomoku decried in her seminal 1960s article "An anthropologist looks at ballet as a form of ethnic dance".[2] The shortage of qualified teaching staff attuned to working in Higher Education and with credibility in the South Asian dance sector has undoubtedly hampered the development of a number of initiatives.[3] Even when properly funded

---

[2] Classifications and categorisations are rarely neutral. They always say something about the ideology of the people who create them. A reflection on the common Western classification of dance into 'folk', 'primitive', 'social', 'art', 'ethnic', for example, demonstrates how contentious these concepts are and how they say more about the ideology of race and class, rooted in 19th century evolutionist theory held by many in contemporary Western societies, than about dance.

positions are available, they do not always get filled. There are people in the South Asian dance community with the right combination of skills and knowledge, but often they have other professional commitments and there are simply not enough of them around.

A number of reports were commissioned in the 1980s and early 1990s to focus on different aspects of South Asian dance in education. They showed clearly that dancers were often treatèd as exotica, expected to provide a whole cultural experience, rather than as dance artists practising highly sophisticated and demanding techniques. Some dancers even mentioned being asked by schools to give cooking demonstrations! As if one would ask Sylvie Guillem to cook *Boeuf Bourguignon* for the students to show something about her French background! It is clear that the dance form itself and the skills of the dancers can be undermined because of underlying, probably unconscious, racist ideology.

Middlesex University and University College Bretton Hall

A new course, leading to a dual *Certificate for Dance Artists in Schools (South Asian Dance)* started in autumn 1995. Developed and validated by Middlesex University and University College, Bretton Hall, it is a step towards bringing the South Asian dance profession and the dance educational system closer together. Designed 'to enable members of the South Asian Dance profession wishing to undertake work in schools, to be more effective and confident within the curricula of primary and secondary education' (Gordziejko, 1995: 1), the course will be an integral part of ADiTi's (the National Organisation of South Asian Dance) educational strategy, relating closely to its objective of establishing South Asian dance within mainstream education.

The proposed certificate is seen as 'a qualification which recognises and accredits the skills of the dancer as teacher . . . [giving dancers] . . . a greater respect within schools and control over their role within an individual session and the curriculum as a whole' (Gordziejko, 1994: 1). By being able to communicate better with teachers, dance artists will 'facilitate a deeper understanding and awareness in staff members, lessening the likelihood of a tokenistic attitude/approach towards the art form' (Turner, 1991: 59).

The course is aimed at students who are already undertaking a career in dance, thus its rationale is seen to be fundamentally different from that of traditional teacher training. Much of the learning process is placed within a working context in which students undertake teaching practices in their own region with a 'mentor'. Students also attend lectures, seminars and group discussions held over six week-ends (three in each institution) during the year.

---

[3]   See, for example, the degree course offered by De Montfort University or the South Asian Dance Teacher Training course at Bedford College (Beattie, 1995: 8; Gordziejko, 1994: 1).

Surrey University

Surrey University has had modules in South Asian dance for many years. The current remodelling of the BA Honours course, renamed *Dance and Culture*,[4] now places South Asian dance on an equal footing with the other dance techniques taught in the programme. The department has chosen initially to concentrate on one technique, Kathak, to allow a more in depth study of a single form.

Kathak is a compulsory subject for all the first year students, taught alongside three other techniques: ballet, a contemporary derived, and an African derived form. Throughout the academic year, students study each style for two hours a week. In the second year, students can choose between two options: concentrating on two out of the four techniques mentioned above, giving them 120 hours for each during the year; or taking a number of short courses of 15 hours duration each, covering a very wide range of dance found within contemporary British society (such as Lambada, or Capoeira, for example). The aim of the courses is to provide future dance workers with some understanding of what they may encounter later in their professional life. It is also argued that by having a broader range of styles taught within the programme, tutors teaching theory classes, such as *Historical Perspectives, Dance and Politics, Concepts of Culture,* or *Critical Perspectives,* have a broader base from which to choose their examples.

What is interesting in such an approach is the development of a stronger ideological base. It promotes a policy of South Asian dance being useful and important for all students, not just those of South Asian origins. Within the *Dance and Culture* programme, in theory at least, Kathak is no less important, or valuable than ballet, for example. However, at Surrey University most technique teachers are "imported" specialists, coming from the professional world into the academic world, and are employed on a "contractual" rather than "permanent" basis. While teachers of Western theatre dance forms find a teaching faculty with a great deal of knowledge about the forms being taught, to give them a support in theory classes, Kathak teachers lack this support. No matter how willing and enthusiastic the other members of staff are, they are not experts in Kathak.

The London Contemporary Dance School

In autumn 1995 a seven week pilot project between the Shobana Jeyasingh Dance Company (SJDC) and the London Contemporary Dance School (LCDS) was set up. Its purpose was to explore the educational and artistic benefits of offering dancers with varied training background, expertise, and experience complementary training in different techniques. It exposed the participants (7 from SJDC and 6 from LCDS) to a range of movement vocabularies, with the aim of stimulating creativity, and exploring varied ways of working and of using the body. The course was

---

[4] It used to be called *Dance in Society.*

conceived in terms of the mutual enrichment of existing dance forms: dancers with a contemporary dance background derived mainly from Graham,
Cunningham, and Limon techniques would be exposed to a modified training in Bharata Natyam technique; dancers with a classical Indian dance training would be exposed to the fundamental training in contemporary and ballet
offered to the first year professional dance students from LCDS. (Scanlon,
1995: 2).

Most of the dancers from LCDS were from the final year of the BA Honours
degree course which required them to explore and reflect on the history and contexts of their chosen art form. Although mostly British dancers trained in contemporary and ballet techniques, they also included an Australian student who had
some experience of Bharata Natyam, and one British Asian student who did not.
All had followed a one term course in Indian dance early on in their training and
some had pursued this interest further by taking extra-curricular classes through
the Academy of Indian Dance.

The dancers from SJDC were a varied group in terms of background, including
British and North American Asian dancers, as well as a dancer from India. Some
of them had previous experience of ballet and contemporary techniques and several had voluntarily undertaken contemporary classes during the LCDS Summer
School prior to the pilot project. All were committed to extending and reflecting
on their own dance experience and knowledge.

The collaborative course involved technical, choreographic, and contextual teachers from LCDS and teachers in Bharata Natyam and Kalari provided by SJDC. In
addition, Shobana Jeyasingh devised and taught a *Choreography and Music* course
together with the composer Alistair MacDonald. In this way the course offered
new technical challenges and creative opportunities to all the dancers involved,
while registering the markedly different training backgrounds and current needs
of the respective participants.

The synthesis of ideas and movement languages resided in the coherence of the
programme as a whole, in the practical, creative and conceptual courses which
students could reflect on and process the material they were encountering in class.
The choreography workshops, above all, were seen to be pivotal in determining
the value of complementary influences, skills and information derived from working with different traditions and culminated in a showing on the last day of the
course.

Although the project was not without its problems, as a whole it was clearly
edifying and stimulating for all involved. The participants had to wrestle with the
various challenges posed, individually and collectively, in a spirit of respect for
each other's skills and knowledge. They unanimously responded enthusiastically.

Comments and Conclusions

Although I had started my enquiry into South Asian dance and Higher Education
with some reservations, worrying about tokenism, I realised that I was partly
mistaken. I found a great many extremely committed individuals who sincerely
believe in the integration of South Asian dance within mainstream dance education. In their views these dance forms should not be promoted simply because
there are persons of South Asian origin living in the country. If this were the case

their value would immediately be debased. Rather they should be perceived as having value in the context of the European tradition because they are novel and technically different systems, with the potential to enrich dance in general.

Yet commitment and enthusiasm are not enough. The extraordinary achievement of Mike Huxley, Naseem Khan and their colleagues, for example, in setting up a full BA combined honour degree in South Asian dance at De Montfort University in 1992, with a full time position to support it, did not lead to the expected wonderful flourishing of South Asian dance studies. Difficulties were experienced in recruiting and retaining staff, and student demand was low with few suitably qualified applicants. Consequently the course is no longer operational.

Why is it so difficult? Clearly the staffing problems are one cause, but there are others which I have alluded to. I firmly believe that the inherent racism found in British society is also to blame. Not blatant, conscious racism, as among National Front supporters, but much more insidious and unconscious forms, existing throughout the community, even among people who defend anti-racist policies with all their heart.

Why is it, for example, that when panels are set up to discuss the implications of the importance the dance cultures of other countries have for dance teaching in general, we often have one panel consisting of 'a choreographer, an eminent teacher, a classical ballerina, a leading contemporary dancer and a distinguished coach and assistant company director' all from within the field of Western theatre dance, and another panel consisting of 'leading representatives of Independent dance, Caribbean dance and South Asian dance' (see the documentation of the 1993 Dance UK Conference). Why the segregation? If they have so much to learn from each other, why keep them apart? Why the use of adjectives such as "eminent" and "distinguished" for one group and not for the other?

Leading choreographers in contemporary dance have been invited to work on South Asian dancers (Richard Alston with SJDC for example) but I am not aware of the reverse taking place. One could argue that the comparatively stronger position that Indian music holds in this country as part of a number of music degree courses, stems from the fact that it has been championed by leading practitioners and that until this happens within the dance profession, South Asian dance will not find the place it deserves.

Working as a lecturer in anthropology, both in dance and non dance contexts I have found that students who do not share mainstream Euro-American cultures are often directed towards anthropology, as if this discipline was somehow more relevant to them. Similarly non-Western dancers tend to be invited to participate in courses which emphasise the community aspects and the socio cultural contexts of dance, rather than its artistic or aesthetic aspects. Aren't these example of insidious racism?

Although the development of courses such as the ones described earlier in this paper is encouraging, we must not sit back complacently but continue pushing for the end of the parochialism Peter Brinson talked about. John Blacking has argued that the whole way of presenting the European tradition must be radically altered, as it was at the times of the Renaissance. New items must not simply be added to the existing syllabi, rather the outlook must become global. As classical Greece and Rome were brought into the orbit of European learning, we must now bring in the cultural achievements of artists, scholars, scientists, engineers, architects and creative individuals and schools from Asia, Africa and other parts of the world (Blacking, 1984). Although this is only a vision for the moment , it is what we must strive for to take us into the next century.

References

Beattie, Theresa (1994) A position paper on Vocational Dance Training in South Asian Dance in Britain. UK

Blacking, John (1984) Dance as a cultural system in Janet Adshead ed. *Dance – a multicultural perspective*, University of Surrey, pp. 17–21

Brinson, Peter (1993) *Dance as education: Towards a national dance culture.* London: The Falmer Press
——— (1994) 'Which way dance teaching? An overview. in Peter Brinson ed. *Tomorrow's dancers: the papers of the 1993 Dance UK Conference 'Training tomorrow's professional dancers'* London: The Laban Centre, pp. 2–7

Gordziejko, Tessa (1994) Certificate for South Asian Dancers Working in Schools, Discussion document from Bretton Hall mini conference 16–17 April 1994. ADiTi
——— (1995) Certificate for South Asian Dancers in Schools Rationale. Middlesex University / University College Bretton Hall

Jeyasingh, Shobana (1994) Training for cultural diversity: South Asian Dance. in Peter Brinson ed. *Tomorrow's dancers: the papers of the 1993 Dance UK Conference 'Training tomorrow's professional dancers'.* London: The Laban Centre pp. 56–57

Keali'inohomoku, Joanne (1969) An anthropologist looks at ballet as a form of ethnic dance. *Impulse*, Marian van Tuyl ed., pp. 24–33 (reprinted in Roger Copeland ed. *What is dance?*)

Maree, Lynn (1992) Opening remarks Proceedings of the South Asian Dance Education Forum. *Choreography and Dance* 3(1): 59–67

Scanlon, Joan (1995) Shobana Jeyasingh/LCDS Pilot Project. London Contemporary Dance School and Jeyasingh Dance Company

Thomas, Helen (1995) *Dance, modernity and culture*, London: Routledge

Turner, Alison (1991) *South Asian Dance in Education Audit.* Bradford: ADiTi Publications

Ward, Andrew (1993) Dancing in the dark: rationalism and the neglect of social dance, in Helen Thomas ed. *Dance, Gender, and Culture.* London: Macmillan, pp. 16–33

Choreography and Dance, 1997, Vol 4(2), pp. 63–66
Reprints available directly from the publisher
Photocopying permitted by license only

South Asian Dance on the Internet: Chris Bannerman in Conversation with Alessandra Iyer

Alessandra Iyer

Christopher Bannerman is Professor of Dance at Middlesex University, where he is head of the School of Dance. Of Canadian origin, he trained in classical ballet and contemporary dance and is a practising dancer and choreographer. A great supporter of South Asian dance, which made an everlasting impression on him when he had the chance to see the great Bharata Natyam dancer Balasaraswati in performance, in 1993 he introduced at Middlesex University a South Asian Dance module. It has been very successful with the students and will continue to be offered in the next academic years.

Christopher Bannerman is very active in the British dance world at different levels. Apart from teaching and performing, he is chair of Dance U.K., trustee of the Academy of Indian Dance, patron of the Language of Dance Centre.

Alessandra Iyer met him at Middlesex University to talk about South Asian dance in education and in performance.

How does South Asian dance figure in your work as choreographer?

It is not an easy question to answer. Many years ago I went to India. It was a very profound experience. I was from Canada, an isolated country, with big open air spaces, and, at least at that time, seemingly culturally uniform. Going to India was a big shock for me in a lot of ways. It put me in touch with a culture that seemed to be extremely . . . long, with a great history to it. An important part of that experience was coming into contact with Indian arts. I had the opportunity to see dance and it was absolutely fascinating. It stayed with me. I did not learn any dance but I saw some performances with Balasaraswati. I felt very privileged in a way; it was simply amazing. I came back to Britain and I began training in contemporary dance and working in choreography. But I did not want to borrow anything in a superficial way. The experience was very profound and gave me an insight into my own culture. I discovered things that had never realised existed. One always takes for granted one's own cultural background until one comes into contact with another culture. So, I cannot say that South Asian dance influenced directly my choreography in the sense of vocabulary, but I was quite interested in some of the concepts. The relationship with music, is one example. I discovered some rhythms in a piece I did about Troubadour songs, 12th century European music. Clearly the rhythmic structure was influenced by the East, yet where that came from is not easy to pinpoint. There was a concept of a rotating rhythm, coming back to one point. The influence was subtle and profound, but not immediately obvious.

Have you ever worked with South Asian dance?

I participated in a work by Subodh Rathod, choreographed using a combination of Bharata Natyam, Kathak and contemporary dance. Unusually for Subodh it followed an issue based theme. He was simply using the forms, juxtaposing them. It was a very short piece but it threw up a lot of possibilities, it is something I would like to return to in the future.

The basic difference between contemporary and South Asian dance is vocabulary and the concept of theatre underpinning this different vocabulary. In some ways that has to do with the way the body moves. Interestingly, unlike music, we, as dancers, have the same instrument, the body, and it is fascinating to see how it can be moved in so many different ways. Seeing how in another culture they control that instrument and the many different vocabularies that are developed, is very challenging. Although I think, for an audience, the transfer of vocabulary and the cross references are obviously very difficult, because of their lack of knowledge, it can occur.

Can South Asian dance be integrated?

Yes. I would probably hesitate to use words such as integrate but, from an artistic point of view, I would say it is not impossible. I guess the artists in future will show us whether it is or not possible. However, the word integration is not right; it is very superficial. It can only be used as shorthand.

There have been past attempts as "integration", "fusion" and so on. Some have not been very successful. Others have. Can you comment?

It is a difficult question, one that should be approached with a feeling of humility. Looking back, many of these attempts appear to be naive and were perhaps based upon incomplete understanding. On the other hand we cannot say that we now have complete understanding either. Perhaps the reason why they did not work, the reason why they look naive, is because we have progressed. Perhaps we have become a little more sophisticated about the concept of culture, developing greater awareness and respect. I hope that is the case. I hope more people can take these things and work with them in a way that is creative and throws up positive feelings.

Take Richard Alston's attempt, for example. I think Richard will agree that it was a very important step, one you learn a lot from and yet needs to be carried further. I found that there were a lot of interesting things as a totality. It threw up all sorts of fascinating comparisons and it set me thinking. What is dance? What is within Western dance tradition? What is within the Indian dance tradition? What does it mean when the two traditions come together? This strand of thought proved fascinating. I would actually like to see the work again. I think Richard found it challenging. I thought he rose to the challenge and the dancers rose to the challenge. Occasionally, you felt that the combination of music and dance, Baroque music and Bharata Natyam, were not quite arriving at the same time, but in its best moments it was wonderful.

Tell me more about your academic role. What did you have in mind when you set up the South Asian dance module?

I would like to refer back to what I said about people not understanding their own cultural base or home until they come into contact with another one. That was the main consideration. Why they feel certain things, why they think some dance and some dancers are good. Clearly, if people are going to be educated in dance there has to be some basis, some understanding of another dance form. South Asian dance offers such a wonderful set of resources for study. You have the *Nāṭyaśāstra*, its very concept is extremely profound. It is important for the students to understand the history of dance as a world activity. Leaping to the present, there are new things that are happening. India as a nation is producing a surge of cultural activity. We have had a spread of Indian culture, South Asian culture. There are many international aspects and developments. In Indian dance these very interesting developments raise all sorts of questions.

Clearly the students are not going to master a new dance vocabulary through this module but they can have an introduction to it. The course has been running for two years now and I would say that it has been extremely successful, the feed back has been very positive. It is not central; it is not the main module, although it can become so in future. It is like planting a seed which hopefully will grow. We are just starting another course, for South Asian dancers who want to work in education, in collaboration with Bretton Hall and ADiTi. I see that, too, as something that can spark off new developments. I am keen on involving everybody.

You are involved with Labanotation to an extent and I also understand that you favour the link between technology and dance. How do you see Labanotation vis à vis South Asian dance and in particular South Asian dance in education? What about computers and dance?

Well, I am not an expert in the area and I am not proficient in any notation system. In Britain currently questions are being asked about the two forms of notation which we have, Laban and Benesh. I think that notation, through technological developments, will become more accessible to people and hence gain in importance. It will become not necessarily easier to learn but easier to use, easier to write. Perhaps it will become possible through computer software to be able to read and translate from one system to the other more easily. That is very important for dance. I think video, notation and computer have a very important role to play. And of course this will not exclude South Asian dance.

I see very clear developments in technology which are changing the experience of dancers. Computers, videos, CD Roms can make dance more accessible. Many people in Britain do not have direct access to South Asian dance. Technology can make it more accessible. It will make the study, the analysis of a particular form much easier. Technology inevitably will have an impact on the form, on the actual art of choreography. When viewed on screen, dance is different and choreographers have to bear this in mind in their work. Perhaps people will soon be able to call up, for example, *Romance with Footnotes* on the Internet. . . . Information technology will bring us, the practitioners, together and will change a lot of things. It will break down the sense of isolation and help to develop connections. And South Asian dance is very much a part of this . . .

Choreography and Dance, 1997, Vol 4(2), pp. 67–71
Reprints available directly from the publisher
Photocopying permitted by license only

© 1997 OPA (Overseas Publishers Association)
Amsterdam B.V. Published in The Netherlands
by Harwood Academic Publishers
Printed in India

LABANOTATED SCORE

THE MAKING OF MAPS
(Excerpts)

Choreographer: Shobana Jeyasingh
Notator: Jean Johnson Jones

Circles

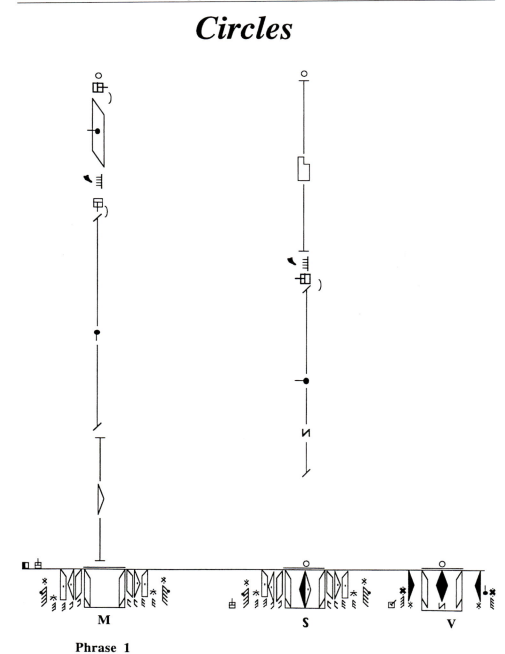

M   **S**   **V**

Phrase 1

Circles

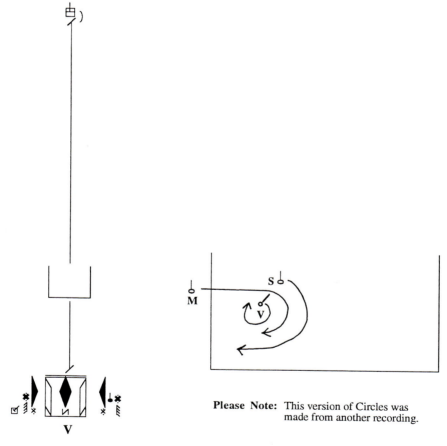

Please Note: This version of Circles was
made from another recording.

Phrase 2

Friends

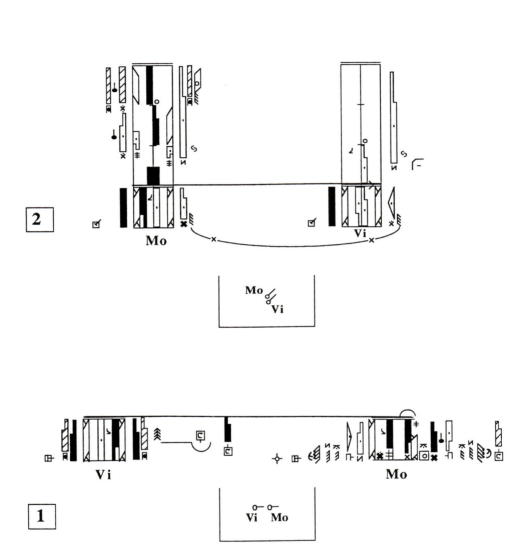

Friends

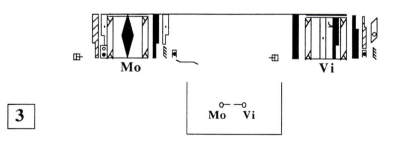

3

Choreography and Dance, 1997, Vol 4(2), pp. 73–75
Reprints available directly from the publisher
Photocopying permitted by license only

THE UGLY DUCKLING
Raga: Bhairavi

Composers: Pandit Vishwa Prakash and Pandit S. Gangani
Notated by Pandit Vishwa Prakash

I

Scene 1 Part A

/SGSG/MGMP/MDDP/MGRN/=2

/NS-R/-G-M/-P-M/GRSR/=2

/SGSG/MGMP/MDDP/MGRN/=2

/NS-R/-G-M/-P-M/GRSR/=2

Antar

/SS-S/-NRS/DP-G/PDS-/=2

/-SSSSSS/-NNNNNN/-DDDDDD/-PPPPPP/=2

2 time

/-RRSSGG/SSRRNNSS/-RRSSGG/SSRRNNSS/=2

2 time

/NN-D/-PGM/GDPM/GRSS/=2

/SGSG/MGMP/MDDP/MGR N =2

Sitar and flute
Tabla and Sinth.
Dub
Tanpura and Santoor

II

Scene 1 Part B
Santoor and Sinth   Raga Bhairavi (Deepchandi)

After two Avartan Jhala

[SSS/RRSS/NNN/SSNN/

/GGG/RRGG/MMG/RRSS] 2
-- Avartan Sinth

[PPP/PPPP/DDD/PPMM/

/DDD/NNSS/DDD/PPMG]2
-- Avartan Sinth

[SSS/RRSS/NNN/SSNN

/GGG/RRGG/MMG/RRSS]2   Santur
                            { Sinth
                              Tabla
                              Tanpura

2 Avartan Sinth

Part C Esraj and Sinth and Harp (Bhairavi + Ektal)

[SS/PP/PM/PN/DP/PP] 2 [/ / / / / /]2 (Harp and Sinth)

[MM/PG/GM/DP/GR/SS]2 [/ / / / / /]2 "   "

[DD/NR/SG/MP/MG/RS] 2 [/ / / / / /] 2 "   "

[DM/MP/NN/RS/ND/PP] 2 [/ / / / / /] 2 "   "

[SS/PP/PM/PN/DP/PP] 2 [/ / / / / /]   Esraj

[GG/MM/DN/SS/NR/RS]2 [/ / / / / /]   Sinth

[PP/PD/PD/PN/DP/GM/]2 [/ / / / / /]   }   Tabla

[DP/MP/NN/RS/ND/PP]2 [/ / / / / /]   Tanpura
                                                       Santoor

Choreography and Dance, 1997, Vol 4(2), pp. 77–78
Reprints available directly from the publisher
Photocopying permitted by license only

© 1997 OPA (Overseas Publishers Association)
Amsterdam B.V. Published in The Netherlands
by Harwood Academic Publishers
Printed in India

Notes on Contributors

Nilima Devi is a Kathak dancer, teacher and choreographer, trained in India. Her Institute of Classical Indian Dance in Leicester, UK, offers a six-year Diploma Course in Kathak dance. Nilima Devi has produced, choreographed and performed many innovative dance pieces, such as *Kathak Katha* (1990), *The Ugly Duckling* (1990, 1992) *Triangle* (1992), *The Rainbow* (1993/94) and *MELORY* (1995).

As part of the annual Leicestershire School Festival, she has contributed extremely successful productions, including *An Evening of Indian Dance* (1987) *Seasons of India* (1989), *Aladdin* (1993), *Stars and Stripes* (1994) and *Togetherness* (1995).

Vena Radha Gheerawo is one of the youngest generation of South Asian dancers trained in Britain. She began dancing at the age of 7 and trained in Bharata Natyam at the Bharatiya Vidya Bhavan, London, under the tutelage of Prakash Yadagudde. She had her arangetram in 1990. Subsequently she won an ADiTi scholarship to train in Bharata Nrityam in Madras under Dr Padma Subrahmanyam, one of the greatest classical dancers of the century and an authority on the obsolete dance of the *Nāṭyaśāstra*. A graduate of the School of Oriental and African Studies, University of London, Vena has taught and performed in Britain and Europe.

Andrée Grau first studied dance in her native Switzerland and later in London at the Dance Centre and the Benesh Institute where she trained in Benesh Movement Notation. She studied with the late Professor John Blacking at The Queen's University of Belfast, obtaining her M.A. in Social Anthropology in 1979 and her Ph.D. in 1983. She has carried out fieldwork among the Venda (South Africa) and among the Tiwi (Northern Australia), as well as in London where she looked at "intercultural" performance within a Western setting. She is currently a Senior Research Fellow in dance at Roehampton Institute. She has written for *Dance Research, Dance Research Journal, Man, Popular Music, Anthropological Forum, Dance Now, The British Journal of Ethnomusicology* and *Visual Anthropology*.

Alessandra Iyer, editor of this issue, is a freelance lecturer and writer on dance and dance iconography. She was awarded a PhD in Art and Archaeology by the School of Oriental and African Studies, University of London, in 1990. She has completed research in India and Indonesia working on the identification and reconstruction of the *karaṇa* of the temple of Śiwa at the Prambanan complex in Central Java. She was for the year 1994 attached to Nrithyodaya, Madras, the institute directed by Dr Padma Subrahmanyam, under the auspices of ICCR (Indian Council for Cultural Relations) and the British Academy. She has contributed papers and articles to a number of journals. Her approach to dance research is both theoretical and practical.

Shobana Jeyasingh was born in Madras, India and spent her childhood in Malaysia and Singapore. She came to Britain in the 1970s. She continued to travel regularly to India in order to complete her Bharata Natyam training under Vallovoor Samraj. After a successful career as a classical soloist, she founded the Shobana Jeyasingh Dance Company of which she is artistic director and choreographer. She has choreographed several works, including: *Raid* (1995), *Romance with Footnotes* (1993), *Making of Maps* (1992), *New Cities Ancient Lands* (1991), *Correspondences* (1990) and *Configurations* (1988). Shobana has choreographed for television and has also worked for the theatre, such as the Royal National Theatre (*The Little Claycart*). Recipient of a MBE for her contribution to dance in Britain, Shobana has been regularly awarded a number of prizes since her company arrived on the scene, including the prestigious Prudential Award for Dance (1993).

Naseem Khan is a freelance writer, arts consultant and administrator, whose 1976 report (*The Arts that Britain Ignore*) opened a debate on cultural diversity. Co-director of the Academy of Indian Dance with Pushkala Gopal in 1980, she has also been coordinator of the British based Festival of India and chair of ADiTi. She trained in Bharata Natyam with the Bangalore couple U.S. Krishna Rao and Chandrabhaga Devi.

Reginald Massey, born in Lahore in undivided India now lives in Wales. His books *The Dances of India* (Tricolour, London) and *The Music of India* (Kahn & Averill, London and Abhinav, New Delhi), written in collaboration with his actress wife Jamilla Massey are well known works. Reginald has been dance critic for *The Dancing Times* for the last 25 years.

Valli Subbiah joined the prestigious Kalakshetra Academy in Madras after completing her schooling in London. She trained in Bharata Natyam for several years under Rukmini Devi. Valli's dance debut was featured in a *"World about us"* documentary on Kalakshetra in 1984. She then joined Kalakshetra Dance Group playing the lead role in many notable dance dramas and earning high praise from dance critics in India and abroad. She also taught at Kalakshetra for several years. Since 1985 she has regularly performed in Britain and Europe touring taditional repertoires such as *Maargam* in 1990 and innovative work such as *The Search* (1989/90). In 1994 Valli formed a company, Sankalpam, together with Mira Balchandran-Gokul and Vidya Thirunarayanan. which toured Britain in 1995 with two pieces, *Alone with themselves* and *Walk around tradition*. Her most recent work was a collaborative project with the Royal Ballet, *Sacred Lands*.

Choreography and Dance, 1997, Vol 4(2), pp. 79–83
Reprints available directly from the publisher
Photocopying permitted by license only

© 1997 OPA (Overseas Publishers Association)
Amsterdam B.V. Published in The Netherlands
by Harwood Academic Publishers
Printed in India

Index

CHOREOGRAPHY AND DANCE
AN INTERNATIONAL JOURNAL

Notes for Contributors

Submission of a paper will be taken to imply that it represents original work not previously published, that it is not being considered for publication elsewhere and that, if accepted for publication, it will not be published elsewhere in the same form, in any language, without the consent of editor and publisher. It is a condition of acceptance by the editor of a typescript for publication that the publisher automatically acquires the copyright of the typescript throughout the world. It will also be assumed that the author has obtained all necessary permissions to include in the paper items such as quotations, musical examples, figures, tables etc. Permissions should be paid for prior to submission.

Typescripts. Papers should be submitted in triplicate to the Editors, *Choreography and Dance, c/o* Harwood Academic Publishers, at:

5th Floor, Reading Bridge House	PO Box 32160	3-14-9, Okubo
Reading Bridge Approach or	Newark, NJ 07102, USA or	Shinjuku-ku
Reading RG1 8PP	+1 800 545 8398	Tokyo 169
UK	+1 201 643 7676	Japan

Papers should be typed or word processed with double spacing on one side of good quality ISO A4 (212 x 297 mm) paper with a 3 cm left-hand margin. Papers are accepted only in English.

Abstracts and Keywords. Each paper requires an abstract of 100–150 words summarizing the significant coverage and findings, presented on a separate sheet of paper. Abstracts should be followed by up to six key words or phrases which, between them, should indicate the subject matter of the paper. These will be used for indexing and data retrieval purposes.

Figures. All figures (photographs, schema, charts, diagrams and graphs) should be numbered with consecutive arabic numerals, have descriptive captions and be mentioned in the text. Figures should be kept separate from the text but an approximate position for each should be indicated in the margin of the typescript. It is the author's responsibility to obtain permission for any reproduction from other sources.

Preparation: Line drawings must be of a high enough standard for direct reproduction; photocopies are not acceptable. They should be prepared in black (india) ink on white art paper, card or tracing paper, with all the lettering and symbols included. Computer-generated graphics of a similar high quality are also acceptable, as are good sharp photoprints ("glossies"). Computer print-outs must be completely legible. Photographs intended for halftone reproduction must be good glossy original prints of maximum contrast. Redrawing or retouching of unusable figures will be charged to authors.

Size: Figures should be planned so that they reduce to 12 cm column width. The preferred width of line drawings is 24 cm, with capital lettering 4 mm high, for reduction by one-half. Photographs for halftone reproduction should be approximately twice the desired finished size.

Captions: A list of figure captions, with the relevant figure numbers, should be typed on a separate sheet of paper and included with the typescript.

Musical examples: Musical examples should be designated as "Figure 1" etc., and the re-commendations above for preparation and sizing should be followed. Examples must be well prepared and of a high standard for reproduction, as they will not be redrawn or retouched by the printer.

In the case of large scores, musical examples will have to be reduced in size and so some clarity will be lost. This should be borne in mind especially with orchestral scores.

Notes are indicated by superior arabic numerals without parentheses. The text of the notes should be collected at the end of the paper.

References are indicated in the text by the name and date system either "Recent work (Smith & Jones, 1987, Robinson, 1985, 1987) . . ." or "Recently Smith & Jones (1987) . . ." If a publication has more than three authors, list all names on the first occurrence; on subsequent occurrences use the first author's name plus "*et al.*" Use an ampersand rather than "and" between the last two authors. If there is more than one publication by the same author(s) in the same year, distinguish by adding a, b, c etc. to both the text citation and the list of references (e.g. "Smith, 1986a") References should be collected and typed in alphabetical order after the Notes and Acknowledgements sections (if these exist). Examples: Benedetti, J. (1988) *Stanislavski,* London: Methuen Granville-Barker, H. (1934) Shakespeare's dramatic art. In *A Companion to Shakespeare Studies,* edited by H. Granville-Barker and G. B. Harrison, p. 84. Cambridge: Cambridge University Press Johnston, D. (1970) Policy in theatre. *Hibernia,* **16**, 16

Proofs. Authors will receive page proofs (including figures) by air mail for correction and these must be returned as instructed within 48 hours of receipt. Please ensure that a full postal address is given on the first page of the typescript so that proofs are not delayed in the post. Authors' alterations, other than those of a typographical nature, in excess of 10% of the original composition cost, will be charged to authors.

Page Charges. There are no page charges to individuals or institutions.

Instructions for Authors

Article Submission on Disk

The Publisher welcomes submissions on disk. The instructions that follow are intended for use by authors whose articles have been accepted for publication and are in final form. Your adherence to these guidelines will facilitate the processing of your disk by the typesetter. These instructions do not replace the journal Notes for Contributors; all information in Notes for Contributors remains in effect.

When typing your article, do not include design or formatting information. Type all text flush left, unjustified and without hyphenation. Do not use indents, tabs or multi-spacing. If an indent is required, please note it by a line space; also mark the position of the indent on the hard copy manuscript. Indicate the beginning of a new paragraph by typing a line space. Leave one space at the end of a sentence, after a comma or other punctuation mark, and before an opening parenthesis. Be sure not to confuse lower case letter "l" with numeral "1", or capital letter "O" with numeral "0". Distinguish opening quotes from close quotes. Do not use automatic page numbering or running heads.

Tables and displayed equations may have to be rekeyed by the typesetter from your hard copy manuscript. Refer to the journal Notes for Contributors for style for Greek characters, variables, vectors, etc.

Articles prepared on most word processors are acceptable. If you have imported equations and/or scientific symbols into your article from another program, please provide details of the program used and the procedures you followed. If you have used macros that you have created, please include them as well.

You may supply illustrations that are available in an electronic format on a separate disk. Please clearly indicate on the disk the file format and/or program used to produce them, and supply a high-quality hard copy of each illustration as well.

Submit your disk when you submit your final hard copy manuscript. The disk file and hard copy must match exactly.

If you are submitting more than one disk, please number each disk. Please mark each disk with the journal title, author name, abbreviated article title and file names.

Be sure to retain a back-up copy of each disk submitted. Pack your disk carefully to avoid damage in shipping, and submit it with your hard copy manuscript and complete Disk Specifications form (see reverse) to the person designated in the journal Notes for Contributors.

DISK SPECIFICATIONS

Journal name _____ Date _____

Paper title _____

_____ Paper Reference Number _____

Corresponding author _____

Address _____

_____

_____ Postcode _____

Telephone _____ Fax _____ E-mail _____

Disks Enclosed (file names and descriptions of contents)

Text   Figures

Disk 1 _____   Disk 1 _____

Disk 2 _____   Disk 2 _____

Disk 3 _____   Disk 3 _____

Computer make and model _____

Size/format of floppy disks

☐ 3.5"   ☐ 5.25"

☐ Single sided   ☐ Double sided

☐ Single density   ☐ Double density   ☐ High density

Operating system _____ Version _____

Word processor program _____ Version _____

Imported maths/science program _____ Version _____

Graphics program _____ Version _____

Files have been saved in the following format

Text: _____

Figures: _____

Maths: _____

PLEASE RETAIN A BACK-UP COPY OF ALL DISK FILES SUBMITTED.

GORDON AND BREACH PUBLISHERS   •   HARWOOD ACADEMIC PUBLISHERS